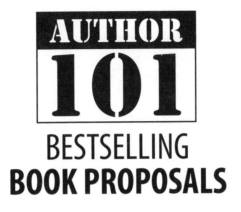

AUTHOR 101

BESTSELLING
BOOK PROPOSALS

The Insider's Guide
to Selling Your Work

Rick Frishman and Robyn Freedman Spizman
with Mark Steisel

Adams Media
Avon, Massachusetts

Published by
Adams Media, an F+W Publications Company
57 Littlefield Street, Avon, MA 02322
www.adamsmedia.com

ISBN: 1-59337-412-7

Printed in the United States of America.

J   I   H   G   F   E   D   C   B   A

Library of Congress Cataloging-in-Publication Data
Frishman, Rick
Author 101—bestselling book proposals : the insider's guide to selling your work /
by Rick Frishman and Robyn Freedman Spizman with Mark Steisel.
p.   cm. — (The author 101 series)
Includes bibliographical references and index.
ISBN 1-59337-412-7 (alk. paper)
1. Book proposals. 2. Authorship—Marketing. I. Spizman, Robyn Freedman.
II. Steisel, Mark. III. Title. IV. Series.
PN161.F747 2005
070.5'2—dc22
2005019807

This publication is designed to provide accurate and authoritative information with
regard to the subject matter covered. It is sold with the understanding that the publisher is not engaged in rendering legal, accounting, or other professional advice. If
legal advice or other expert assistance is required, the services of a competent professional person should be sought.
      —From a *Declaration of Principles* jointly adopted by a Committee of the
American Bar Association and a Committee of Publishers and Associations

Many of the designations used by manufacturers and sellers to distinguish their products are claimed as trademarks. Where those designations appear in this book and
Adams Media was aware of a trademark claim, the designations have been printed
with initial capital letters.

This book is available at quantity discounts for bulk purchases.
For information, please call 1-800-872-5627.

All it takes to get a book published is getting one person to say "yes." We dedicate this book to the editors, publishers, and individuals along the way who said "yes" to us and hopefully will say "yes" to you too.

■ ■ ■

To my wife, Robbi, with love and thanks.
—*Rick Frishman*

To my husband, Willy, and our children, Justin and Ali.
You make life a bestseller!
—*Robyn Freedman Spizman*

Contents

Foreword

THIS BOOK WAS one of the exciting by products of my MEGA Book Marketing University. I couldn't be happier or prouder about it, or more delighted to write the foreword. Since 1993, my good friend Rick Frishman has designed and managed the publicity campaigns for all my books, and in recent years, he's become the star public relations instructor at MEGA. Rick's coauthor, Robyn Spizman, is a talented author, seasoned media personality, and cofounder of the Spizman Agency, a well-known public relations agency in Atlanta that oversees one of the nation's top author and leading-edge thinker's programs at which I have been featured; she has also sat on panels and participated in educational programs at MEGA. Right off the bat, you have two superstars from this business.

In 2004, Rick invited Scott Watrous, Chief Operating Officer of Adams Media, and Gary Krebs, Publishing Director of Adams, to be his guests at MEGA. The experience opened their eyes, and subsequently, Rick's, Robyn's, and mine as well. Scott and Gary saw that though the would-be authors who attended MEGA had tremendous passion, enthusiasm, and ability, what many of them lacked was an intricate knowledge of how to write book proposals, get a literary agent, and promote their books.

Scott and Gary sat down with Rick and Robyn, who had been working on a concept that they had titled "Author 101," and brain-stormed. When four people that smart put their heads together, you know something good's going to come about—and it did. That weekend, those four people developed the vision for the program that you are about to begin.

The goal of *Author 101* is very simple and direct: to take novice authors and give them a grounding in the business of writing that matches their talent and commitment. For instance, in *Bestselling Book Proposals*, Rick and Robyn have produced a wealth of material on writing a book proposal from an insider's perspective—that is, from the point of view of people who have not only written book proposals, but have evaluated those written by others. Their wisdom is invaluable to anyone who aspires to be a published author, because as we all know, in any business, talent is not enough. You've got to be smart. And with the *Author 101* program, you'll get smart. You'll learn the inside tips and tricks that make a proposal stand out from the thousands of others like it, make a book more attractive to a publisher, generate millions in free publicity, and a lot more.

I love this book and the entire *Author 101* concept because I see the same need that Scott, Gary, Rick, and Robyn saw at MEGA: a lot of eager people with great ideas but without that practical foundation in the business of publishing that helps successful authors become successful. By the end of the weekend, I could sense the confusion, and it was really a call for help. Well, Rick and Robyn have answered that call. As the *Author 101* series continues, they'll be debuting a second book, *Bestselling Secrets from Top Agents*. They'll also be starting a series of educational seminars—as well as teleconferences, if you're unable to drop everything and get on a plane—featuring some of the top agents, publishers, editors, and writers in the industry. The goal is always the same: to help you become a better, smarter writer and a more salable, prosperous author.

Can you benefit from *Author 101: Bestselling Book Proposals* if you've already been published? Sure. After all, there's no such thing as too much knowledge. Even if you've already sold and marketed your first book, or if you've self-published, you can always learn more about writing great proposals and marketing plans, doing better competitive research, or creating chapter outlines that get agents making excited 2 A.M. phone calls.

However, *Author 101* is really all about the first-time writer. If you've always felt like there was a book inside you just fighting to get out, if you want to write a book to jumpstart your current career or vector off into a new one, and if you have a brilliant idea but don't know how to sell or market it, *Author 101* is your complete, soup-to-nuts resource. When it comes to learning how to write, sell, and promote your book from start to finish, you can't do better than Rick and Robyn. I know. That's why I've chosen to work with them for many years.

So take a deep breath and dive into *Bestselling Book Proposals*. I think you'll learn more than you ever thought possible about what it takes to get your book noticed by the publishing industry. More important than that, you'll pick up ideas and develop skills that will make you a better, more marketable, more business-savvy author. And as someone who loves helping writers turn their dreams into wonderful books, I can't think of a better result.

So what are you waiting for? There are proposals to be written!

Aim high and achieve higher,

—Mark Victor Hansen,
co-creator of the *Chicken Soup for the Soul* series

Acknowledgments

ONE OF THE GREATEST PLEASURES of working with books and publishing is the marvelous, intelligent people we have had the pleasure of meeting. Our workdays have been made brighter and more enjoyable because we have been fortunate enough to work with such outstanding individuals. For that, we count our blessings and give our thanks.

To begin, our warmest thanks to Gary Krebs and Scott Watrous of Adams Media, who gave us the green light when we presented this book series. Their steadfast enthusiasm for the project and encouragement has lit a fire under us. Thank you also Paula Munier, our editor, for your help and guidance. And thanks to our development editor Larry Shea and to all of the wonderful staff at Adams Media for all the great work you have done on our behalf.

To our many and gifted literary contacts, thanks for your help! When we contacted them to help us with this book, our friends consistently came through and shared their amazing insights with us. Experts who had also authored books on book proposals generously offered their time and knowledge to us, and for that we are truly grateful! We learned so much from them, and their generous contributions formed the guts of our book.

Therefore, we would like to give our heartfelt thanks to all of you who have given so much to us and to this book. We are extremely grateful! We would like to especially acknowledge and thank the following individuals.

Andree Abecassis
Jill Alexander
Peter Applebome
Ken Atchity
Liv Bloomer
Bonnie Bock
Susan Burke
Leanne Chearney
Danielle Chiotti
June Clark
Roger Cooper
Jenny Corsey
Richard Curtis
Jennifer Enderlin
Debra W. Englander

Grace Freedson
Guy Garcia
Don Gastwirth
Stedman Graham
Marion Gropen
Tim Hayes
Tory Johnson
Jeremy Katz
Edward W. Knappman
Gary M. Krebs
Ronald E. Laitsch
Michael Larsen
Jay Conrad Levinson
Bonnie Marson
Sharlene Martin

Michael McLaughlin
Peter Miller
Gene Molter
John Monteleone
Paula Munier
Diane Reverand
Steven Schragis
Sara Slavin
Bonnie Solow
Willy Spizman
Carolyn Turknett
Dr. Robert Turknett
Dr. Ava Wilensky
John Willig
Stephen Yafa

We also wish to pay homage and express our great appreciation to the book world's literary gurus, those pioneering individuals who paved the way for all of us through their outstanding efforts. These superheroes blazed the trail and showed us—and so many others—that we could fulfill our dreams of being published authors. With that said, we wish to thank Jack Canfield, Mark Victor Hansen, Bill and Steve Harrison, Jeff Herman, John Kremer, Michael Larsen, Jan Nathan, Dan Poynter, and Marilyn Ross, as well as many others, too numerous to mention, who have devoted their careers to helping aspiring authors succeed. It is with deep appreciation that we salute them for sharing their knowledge and their dedication to writing and publishing.

From Robyn: To my wonderful family—my husband, Willy, and our children, Justin and Ali. You fill my life with laughter and love. To my parents, Phyllis and Jack Freedman, who have cheered me on to success. To my brother Doug who said, "Real authors have agents." To Genie, Sam, and Gena and my devoted family and wonderful group of friends. To my dear friend, Ava Wilensky, who said I must write a book series on getting published, and a special thanks to the Spizman Agency, Jenny Corsey, and Bettye Storne for your unending devotion and support.

To my coauthor Rick Frishman, who is genuinely one of the finest human beings on this planet. Thank you, Rick, for being such a remarkable friend and coauthor. And to the talented Mark Steisel, who is a total literary genius in our book!

Thanks also to Meredith Bernstein for steadfast friendship and expert literary guidance throughout the years. To Ron and Mary Lee Laitsch, for your belief in me, and to my readers, who continue to grace me with their presence. I am most fortunate to have all of you in my life.

From Rick: The first thank-you goes to my wonderful coauthor, Robyn Spizman who I've known for over twenty years and is one of the finest coauthors a guy could ask for.

Mark Steisel—your help and wisdom have been invaluable. Working with you has been a joy.

Thank you to our super editor at Adams Media, Paula Munier, and to Gary Krebs and, of course, the man who made this happen, Scott Watrous. Thank you, Beth Gissinger, publicity guru at Adams, for all of your hard work.

I have to acknowledge Mike (Manny) Levine, who founded Planned Television Arts in 1962 and was my mentor, and partner for over eighteen years. Mike taught me that work has to be fun and meaningful and then the profits will follow.

To my exceptional management team at PTA—David Hahn, David Thalberg, and Sandy Trupp—your professionalism, loyalty, and friendship means more to me than you will ever know. To Hillary Rivman, who helped build PTA and is still an affiliate and friend of our company. To Bob Unterman—you are always there when I need you and are truly a best friend. To the staff of PTA, you are the best in the business.

Thank you to David and Peter Finn, Tony Esposito, Richard Funess, and all of my colleagues at Ruder Finn. It is an honor to be part of this amazing company.

To my friends Mark Victor Hansen and Jack Canfield. Making the journey with the two of you has been incredible, and your friendship and advice have been invaluable.

To Harvey Mackay: For the lessons about networking and for your amazing support. You are in a class of your own.

To my mother and father, for keeping me out of the fur business and helping me discover my own destiny. And to my brother Scott, who has always been there to support me in whatever I do.

To my children Adam, Rachel, and Stephanie. Watching you grow into fine young individuals has been the highlight of my life. And to my wife, Robbi—you are my strength.

Introduction

Welcome to *Author 101: Bestselling Book Proposals.*

First, let us begin by telling you why we wrote this book. Both of us have spent most of our adult lives working with books, publishing, and writers; books have been our careers and burning interest. We love books and writing and they've clearly been good to us.

As frequently published authors, we know the wonders of writing and publishing books. We've experienced the joy of seeing our books in stores, on Amazon.com, and in our friends' homes. We know how glorious and fulfilling it is to express what we know, especially when it helps others. It's made us feel proud and worthwhile. There's little like it! We hope that this book helps you share those special pleasures.

Over the years, we've worked with hundreds and hundreds of the best writers, agents, editors, and publishers. We've talked frequently with them about books, writing, and publishing. Together, we've planned, strategized, and struggled to meet deadlines. We've celebrated with each other when our projects worked and commiserated when they flopped.

We know the industry, what it's about and how it works. Most of all, we understand that writing a book isn't easy and that getting it published can be even harder. We also know that many wonderful writers are out there who should be heard. So, we want to help.

Before we go any further, let us tell you about ourselves, who we are, why we're qualified to write this book, and why we think you should read it.

Rick's Story

I've been handling publicity for authors since 1976. In 1982, I became the president of Planned Television Arts, which is now one of the world's top firms specializing in publicizing and promoting books. In addition, I serve as an executive vice-president at Ruder Finn, the largest PR firm in New York. I am also the coauthor of three previous books, *Guerrilla Marketing for Writers*, *Guerrilla Publicity,* and *Networking Magic.*

During my career, I've personally handled thousands of publicity campaigns for books by famous authors and authors who wanted to become famous. Some of the names of my clients that you will recognize are former President Jimmy Carter, Vice President Dick Cheney, Presidential Advisor Henry Kissinger, Duchess of York Sarah Ferguson, U.S. Senator John Glenn, former Education Secretary William Bennett, Foreign Minister of Israel Shimon Peres, Walt Disney CEO Michael Eisner, Charles Schwab Brokerage founder Charles Schwab, Wendy's CEO Dave Thomas, Virgin Airlines CEO Richard Branson, Harvey Mackay, Arnold Palmer, Lance Armstrong, Elton John, Wolfgang Puck, Joan Rivers, Rev. Robert Schuller, Ben Stiller, Drew Barrymore, Wynton Marsalis, Naomi Judd, Charlton Heston, Paul Reiser, Sandra Bullock, and hundreds more.

I always dreamed of becoming an author, but I though it was something that I would never achieve. My writer clients showed me, firsthand, the rewards and satisfactions of being an author, which I dreamed of for myself. However, I was always on the outside. Then, Michael Larsen, the San Francisco literary agent, asked me to work with him and Jay Conrad Levinson in cowriting the book *Guerrilla Marketing for Writers* (Writer's Digest Books, 2001), and I jumped at the chance. Finally, I had the opportunity to make my dream of being an author come true.

As we worked on my first book, I found that I had things to say and to teach others. When the book came out, people were responsive and I saw that I could really help. Helping others fulfill their dreams gave me enormous satisfaction; it made me feel great.

Shortly after *Guerrilla Marketing for Writers* was released, Jill Lublin, a California publicist, invited me to team up with her and Jay Conrad Levinson on *Guerrilla Publicity* (Adams Media, 2002), which, of course,

I did. It gave me the opportunity to teach a wide audience about publicity and how individuals can get publicity on their own. *Guerrilla Publicity* became a big hit and I was hooked. I loved being an author and helping people . . . plus, it created an even closer bond with my clients because it gave me a fuller appreciation of their work.

As an author, I've found that if your book is relatively successful and you have a platform, your publisher will want more books from you—and I've been delighted to comply. *Guerrilla Publicity* was followed by *Networking Magic* and, now, this new series of four Author 101 books. Once you have a book out, a funny thing happens: You want to do it again and again. Although writing a book is lots of work, the rewards are sensational. It's exciting, exhilarating and uplifting when your book is about to be published, when you first see it in the publisher's catalog, when you see it in the bookstores and when you go to sign books.

I hope that the information in *Author 101: Bestselling Book Proposals* will help you get your book published. The world needs new voices, new stories, and new teachers, and you may be able to fill the bill. Work hard, follow the advice in this book, learn all about publishing and book proposals, and I'll look forward to seeing you on the shelf.

Robyn's Story

Since 1981, I have been consumed with the world of books. I have now written and coauthored dozens of books. Sounds crazy, but over two decades ago, I retired from teaching elementary school art to have our first child, Justin. A fellow educational resource director, Howard Knopf, recommended me to Good Apple Publishers (which was later purchased by Simon & Schuster) when asked if he knew any teachers who would be candidates to write a book. While I had no clue at that time how to write a book, I was a quick study and found nonfiction writing to be an ideal match. I became the queen of catchy captions and clever phrases and went on to write many educational books for teachers and also how-to craft books, since a well-known craft publisher was also looking for creative book ideas. I had found my niche—my calling was clear.

When my first craft book came out, a new talk show in Atlanta, called *Noonday*, was starting on the NBC affiliate WXIA-TV. I called up and introduced myself because they were featuring authors. While my books were small and a far cry from works of literary genius, they were still books. And teachers and crafters appreciated them. And I believed I was an author and wanted to promote my books and share my knowledge. To this day, I count those initial books as the stepping-stones to my literary accomplishments.

However, the turning point for my entire career occurred at a family dinner when my older brother Doug said, "Real authors have agents." So, the following week, I called a well-known author in Atlanta, who agreed. Though foreign to me, I did what most teachers do when they don't know something. I went to the library and researched how to find a literary agent.

There, I found a huge book called *Books in Print,* which listed every publisher and publishing contact. Because it is a reference book and can't be checked out, I wrote down the name of the Meredith Bernstein Literary Agency and another gentleman's name on my checkbook register and made the call. The gentleman quickly entertained my call and wanted to meet with me. Hold on, I thought, that was too easy. But then I called Meredith Bernstein, who asked me really thoughtful, provoking questions about my previous books and what I wanted to write about. Then, a light bulb went off. As luck would have it, I was going to New York City for a trip, and my husband and I met with her. A few hours later, I was on my way to meet with publishers, which astounded me. It was a whirlwind, but I was confident I could do it.

Those meetings and that stack of craft and educational books, where I paid my dues (and I might add, I loved every second of writing those books), led to my first trade book, which was called *Lollipop Grapes and Clothespin Critters* (imagine that name as your credit to literary fame), and my trade nonfiction career was born. I was hooked. As our toddler Justin unplugged every electrical cord in the house, I wondered what I needed to know to be the most effective parent on earth. So, I approached a child psychologist and his wife, Drs. Stephen and

Marianne Garber, and together we wrote *Good Behavior, Monsters Under the Bed, Beyond Ritalin,* and other books that became very well-received parenting books. I also began writing inspirational and consumer advocacy books, as I was reporting weekly on a variety of topics as Super Mom and the Super Shopper on TV.

Call me a book-a-holic . . . but I caught the book-writing bug.

To date I have written more books than I ever dreamed and am still going strong—from *The Thank You Book, When Words Matter Most* to *The GIFTionary* to *Make It Memorable.* Plus, I've written a series of Women For Hire books with my gifted coauthor and nationally recognized career expert, Tory Johnson, CEO and founder of Women For Hire, including *Women For Hire: The Ultimate Guide to Getting a Job* and *The Get-Ahead Guide to Career Success.* It's been a meaningful journey.

And just when I thought I'd never become the children's book author that I dreamed about being, I most recently launched my first children's novel, which I coauthored with the talented Mark Johnston, titled *Secret Agent.* Yes, the journey to becoming an author and discovering my talents and voice has been an eventful and meaningful one.

I love being an author. I love waking up in the morning and bringing ideas to life. I adore the chase, the challenge, the ups (not always the downs), the unknown. When you become an author, you open up a door to worlds you never knew existed inside you. Yet, the world also becomes a small, intimate gathering of friends and you find yourself connected to something grand. I am honored to call myself an author, and hope to share the gifts of our know-how with you.

Now, let's get started. There is much to learn, and we have work to do!

The Publishing Mystique

Publishing is a unique and mysterious universe, unlike most businesses in which you may have been involved. It's a maze, and many insiders strive to maintain the mystique. To help you find your way, we've written this book. It's meant to be practical, to give tons of timely, insightful tips to authors who are searching for instant answers, answers to questions that we've faced countless times and had to learn, sometimes painfully, how to figure out.

Let's cut to the chase!

This book is written for today's writers, individuals who live in fast-paced times and don't have the time or patience to read long-winded books on getting published. It's for both aspiring and established writers who just want answers—to learn the ropes and get the inside scoop on what other authors and experts know. It's intended to give them information that will enable them to come off like pros, avoid the unknowns and land big book deals.

We specifically designed this book to address the major question we've been asked for decades: "How can I get my book published?" To get that information, we asked top editors, agents, and publishing professionals. So what you will read comes right from insiders who know. While many books address the universe of publishing, this book gives you the inside information you need to start collecting royalties. *Bestselling Book Proposals* won't just give you the ABCs of writing book proposals; it will cover the entire alphabet.

Please feel free to contact us at *www.author101.com* with your comments, questions, and suggestions. We would also love to hear from you about your own book proposal experiences.

Enjoy this book!

—Rick Frishman and Robyn Freedman Spizman

CHAPTER

1

"You don't write because you want to say something: You write because you've got something to say."

F. Scott Fitzgerald

Insider Facts about the Publishing Industry

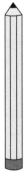

THIS CHAPTER WILL COVER:

▶ Publishing is a business
▶ Publishing facts
▶ Industry players
▶ Traditional structure

WE'RE EXCITED THAT you want to become a published author, and we've dedicated this book to help you reach that goal. The road to publication can be bumpy, indirect, and confusing. Many writers find that they need a guide. That's why we've written this book: to give you vital information that you will need and to show you the best routes, short cuts, and approaches to smooth your way.

The competition to get books published is fierce; it seems like everyone wants to write and publish a book. To increase your odds of making the cut, we've filled this book with information we've learned throughout our careers working in the book business, and added insights provided by top experts. From the get-go, we want you to understand what's involved in getting your book published, what you're getting into, and precisely what you have to do. The world of books is magical and mysterious. Publishing is a special universe. When you try to move inside and work your way through the publishing process, it can be daunting. Newcomers can easily get lost, swallowed up, and discouraged. Seasoned authors can grow frustrated, angry, and disillusioned. Writers at all levels, from unpublished novices to successful veterans, need help finding their way. That's why we're here, to show you what to do.

For starters, understand that the publishing industry is complex and can be baffling. It's riddled with rules, most of which are unwritten and difficult to decode. The rules were made by publishers, and guess whom they benefit? Why, publishers of course. The rules give publishers the upper hand.

The publishing industry is filled with insiders: mainly editors, literary agents, booksellers, and publishing company personnel. Most others, including writers, are kept out. Publishing insiders speak their own language, which makes outsiders feel lost. Many of the rules are inside secrets that are based on old traditions and protocols. The rules may differ from agent to agent, editor to editor, and publisher to publisher. Plus, they can change instantly at the drop of a corporate memo or on a bigwig's whim.

Publishing is a mysterious world that constantly changes. It follows and reacts to the media, trends, and the news. Recently, the industry has gone through major consolidation that has left it with a handful of major publishers and thousands of smaller-sized firms. Due to corporate takeovers and consolidation, this industry, which was once devoted to the art of fine writing, now primarily worships the bottom line.

As an industry, publishing is in mortal combat for consumer dollars with the makers of motion pictures, radio, television, video games, computers, recorded music, sporting events, and others. It's also in the clutches of a small group of mega booksellers who have the market clout to influence, if not dictate, what books are published. To make matters worse, publishing operates under an archaic system under which booksellers may return unsold books for full refunds.

If you hope to be a published writer, it's crucial for you to know the rules of the game and the layout of the field before you try to play. Without such knowledge, you don't stand much of a chance. If you want to get your manuscript published, it's crucial for you to understand as much as possible about those you hope to impress: the publishing establishment and especially editors, agents, and publishing houses. At the least, you should know:

- Who they are.
- Precisely what they do.
- Exactly what they want.
- How you can best fit in.

Publishing Is a Business

When writers try to sell their books, many start at a disadvantage because they place the book publishing business on a pedestal. They tend to romanticize the industry and approach it with stars in their eyes. Often, they wrap all their hopes in their books, which they see as lofty endeavors that will launch their literary careers and fulfill their dreams. In doing so, they often project qualities on publishing companies that simply don't exist. They may think that because publishing deals with arts, letters, and culture, the industry operates on a higher plane or its major concern is art and beauty, which certainly isn't true.

In the following pages, we're going to demystify book publishing and explain how it works. We're going to pass on to you the cumulative wisdom of top experts in the field, experts who know all the secrets, the ins and outs, and can explain exactly what you must know. This information will give you a decided advantage in getting your book published.

LESSON #1
BOOK PUBLISHING IS A BUSINESS!

If you get nothing else from this book, understand that publishing is a business; a big business that is bottom-line oriented. Publishing companies need to make profits to survive. Virtually every major decision made in the publishing industry is filtered through a business, profit-oriented lens. Publishers are business operators who deal in the commodity of books.

While many publishing companies have high artistic standards, they are not charities or benevolent associations. They are not cultural foundations that exist solely to serve writers and the public good; they are businesses that exist to make money.

Publishing Facts

- Publishers love to find exciting new authors.
- However, publishers are not first and foremost in the talent-discovery business.
- Publishers are primarily in the money-making business and most try to make it artfully.

As an author, you may have an idea for the most interesting, brilliant, or even earth-shattering book. Your writing skill may move curmudgeons to tears or goad the meek to destructive outbursts. However, if publishers don't think your work is commercial, you'll have trouble getting it through their acquisition processes.

How big a business is publishing? According to statistics compiled by industry expert Dan Poynter (as he states on his Web site at *http:// parapublishing.com/statistics*), book sales totaled approximately $26.9 billion in 2002 (Source: Association of American Publishers, *www. publishers.org/industry/index.cfm*). This amounted to a 5.5 percent increase over 2001 (*Publishers Weekly*, March 10, 2003, *www.PublishersWeekly.com*). When the total number of books published in 2004 is finally counted, it's projected to exceed 175,000. So, as you can see, publishing is a huge business. As a writer, it's essential to always remember that when publishing decisions are made, they will usually be based primarily on dollars-and-cents business considerations, not on art!

Industry Players

In the past decade or so, the publishing industry has been confronted with powerful new competitors. For example, mountains of information and entertainment now stream into readers' homes as a result of the emergence of the Internet and the explosive expansion of cable television. Access has become easy and virtually universal because it leapfrogs boundaries. In the process, it's changed the culture.

Simultaneously, the book-publishing industry has gone through massive changes. It has consolidated dramatically. Imprints that were formerly rivals are now sister companies and partners. Standardized, corporate organizational practices have replaced looser, more hands-on, family-oriented operations. Book publishing has also benefited from waves of technical innovations that have impacted virtually every aspect of the business, including how books are printed, distributed, and sold.

Picture today's book-publishing industry as a sharply pointed triangle. The narrow top of the triangle contains a handful of players, while the bottom portion is densely packed. As the triangle rises, the mass of publishing companies thins.

Six huge, multinational conglomerates dominate the book-publishing business; together, they put out about 80 percent of all books sold. Four of these giants are foreign owned, but all have headquarters in New York City, which is the world book-publishing center. As a

> "Understand the business realities of publishing and keep them prominently in mind through *every stage* of the book-selling and publishing process: idea formation, proposal writing, agent/publisher selection/interaction, manuscript development, submission, and promotion. Find out what agents and publishers want and make your writing more attractive to them by giving them what they request. Otherwise, the public will probably never get the chance to appreciate your genius."

result, the big six are considered "New York Publishers," which carries a certain literary cachet, even though they're actually owned by corporations based in Munich, London, or Sydney.

The six publishing colossi are:

1. **Random House, Inc.**, a division of Bertelsmann AG (a German corporation), is the world's largest English-language general trade book publisher. It publishes some seventy imprints, including Anchor, Ballantine, Bantam, Broadway, Crown, Dell, Del Rey, Dial, Doubleday, Fawcett, Fodor, Dell, Knopf Group, Pantheon, Random House, Villard, and Vintage. It also owns the Literary Guild.

2. **The Penguin Group**, which is owned by Pearson (United Kingdom), is the second-largest publisher in the United States and Canada and the largest in the United Kingdom, Australia, New Zealand, and India. Its imprints include Allen Lane, Avery, Berkley Books, Dutton, Hamish Hamilton, Michael Joseph, Plume, Putnam, Riverhead, and Viking. Penguin also publishes children's brands such as Puffin, Ladybird, Dutton, and Grosset & Dunlap.

3. **HarperCollins**, a subsidiary of the News Corporation Limited (Australia), has annual revenues of over $1 billion. Its imprints include Amistad, Avon, Caedmon, Ecco, Eos, HarperBusiness, HarperCollins, HarperSanFrancisco, Perennial, Rayo, ReganBooks, and William Morrow. Its Zondervan unit publishes Bibles and Christian books, and its e-book imprint is PerfectBound.

4. **Holtzbrinck Publishing Holdings** (Germany), publishes imprints that include Argon; Farrar, Straus & Giroux; Hanley & Belfus; Henry Holt; Hill & Wang; Macmillan; North Point Press; Picador; St. Martin's; Scientific American; Times Books (partnership with New York Times Group); and Urban & Fischer.

5. **Time Warner Book Group Inc.** (United States) owns the Book-of-the-Month Club and the imprints Aspect; Back Bay; Bulfinch; Little, Brown and Company; Press Warner Books, the Mysterious Press, and Warner Books (Warner Business Books, Warner

Faith, and Warner Vision). It also distributes publishing lines for Hyperion, Arcade, Disney, Harry Abrams, Time-Life Books, and Microsoft.

6. **Simon & Schuster, Inc.**, is the publishing arm of Viacom (United States). It publishes Aladdin Paperbacks, Atheneum, Atria, Fireside, the Free Press, Little Simon, MTV Books, Margaret K. McElderry, Pocket Books, Scribner, Simon & Schuster, Simon Spotlight, Star Trek, Touchstone, Washington Square Press, and Wall Street Journal Books.

A seventh biggie is **Disney Publishing Worldwide** (United States), a subsidiary of the entertainment giant the Walt Disney Company. It publishes ABC Daytime Press, ESPN Books, Hyperion, Miramax, and Theia.

In addition to the giant publishers, Dan Poynter reports that some 300 to 400 medium-sized publishers exist, along with more than 85,000 small and self-publishers. With the explosion in electronic books, printing on demand, and other innovations, the field continues to expand.

What You Need to Know

So, how do the changes in publishing affect you? Since information and entertainment are so readily available, publishers have become more selective. The books they publish must be better than what readers can get online or on TV.

Industry consolidation has created fewer publishers/buyers, which could make it harder for you to capture a big publisher's attention. This translates into more competition for you from other authors. It probably means that your proposal will be evaluated on a strict dollars-and-cents basis or that you will have to comply with a bunch of rigid, corporate-imposed demands. It could also limit your flexibility as a writer and your input into the way your book is designed, marketed, and promoted.

Some writers find smaller, even local publishers in their area easier to approach and more accommodating. So when you start identifying potential publishers for your masterpiece, don't just look at the big guys. Be open to all publishers and pay special attention to those who have published books like the one you wish to write. Your publisher just might be in your own backyard! Do some homework.

"The publishing industry has become more and more a business driven by hits," legendary New York City literary agent Richard Curtis (of Richard Curtis Associates, Inc.) explains. "It's like music, movies, and the media; it's more and more a business for stars. People who want to enter are finding the bar has been raised higher and higher and their options are more limited." So writers who hope to be published must find ways to get into the system, and that usually requires them to increase their profiles.

The Publishing Process

For the purposes of this book, let's look at book publishing as having three major components. They are:

WRITERS >>> LITERARY AGENTS >>> PUBLISHERS

Naturally, many others are involved in the book-publishing process, including editors, indexers, designers, production specialists, printers, sales personnel, publicists, warehousers, and shippers. And let's not forget booksellers. However, for our purposes, let's just look at the basic three.

Publishing a book is a long, complex, arduous, exacting, and expensive process. According to industry figures, 80 percent of the books published fail. One percent of all books sold account for 50 percent of all publishing company profits. It takes large publishing houses a year to two years to put out a book, and the average cost is $50,000 per title.

Ideally, we would like to think that writers, literary agents, and publishers are coequal partners that each carry an equivalent load and

have the same importance. However, in reality, that's not how it works. In book publishing, a pecking order definitely exists, and the playing field is certainly not level. The differences are based on power. Publishers sit at the top above agents, and then writers.

Writers

Writers are the miners who descend into the depths to extract the basic ore that hopefully will turn out to be pure gold. They dig out the words and shape them into the content that feeds the publishing machine. Publishers take writers' efforts, polish and refine them, package them into attractive formats, and distribute them. They're also supposed to promote their books, but they don't always do a very good job.

In the beginning of the publishing process, during the courtship period, a talented author who has something to say reigns supreme. Publishers and agents will covet and compete for talented authors.

In order to interest a publisher, writers—at the least—must show that they have:

- An idea or approach that readers are likely to buy.
- The talent, dedication, and discipline to write and deliver a book on time.
- The desire and ability to promote and support book sales.

A writer must convince a publisher that his or her book will justify the large expenditures that the publisher must make.

Fiction versus Nonfiction

Books fall into two primary categories: fiction and nonfiction. Although the line separating them has been blurred, nonfiction is basically writing that discusses facts and actual events. Categories of nonfiction include history, psychology, philosophy, how-to, and explanatory works.

Fiction is writing that is not necessarily based on facts or events. In fiction, the facts or events may be invented, changed, or further developed. A fictional book may be built on actual events around which imaginary scenarios have been created. Examples of fiction include novels, short stories, and plays.

The usual way nonfiction writers, especially those with no track records, attract publishers' attention is by submitting book proposals. The vast majority of nonfiction books are bought on the basis of proposals. In this book, we will concentrate primarily on proposals for nonfiction books.

Proposals don't play the same role with works of fiction, especially for first-time authors. With fiction, agents and editors usually want to see the entire manuscript so they can assess the quality of the story and the author's writing. So first-time novels and books of short stories and poetry are usually sold on the basis of a manuscript that the writer submits. Proposals do come into play for fiction writers when they want to sell subsequent fictional books.

First-time fiction writers should send queries to editors and agents that include an outline, a synopsis of their work, and sample chapters of the completed manuscript. In most cases, agents and editors prefer to read as much of fictional works as possible so they can make more informed acquisition decisions. Check with each agent and publisher to clarify exactly how much of your writing they want you to submit.

Many publishers won't accept unsolicited manuscripts or proposals. Those that will, frequently toss them into what the industry calls the slush pile. Since so many writers hope to be published, slush piles usually climb to intimidating heights.

At publishing houses that accept unsolicited submissions, the most junior editors are assigned to read the manuscripts in slush piles.

Usually, these editors are new hires who are often just out of school. They may be brilliant or even prescient, but they're usually pretty inexperienced, and they're always overworked and underpaid. So in most cases, your masterpiece will probably be read, or more likely skimmed, by a totally exhausted, bleary-eyed, irritable novice . . . at best. It's not a pretty picture.

Although some literary agencies and publishing houses take pride in pulling gems from the slush, success via that route is a real long shot.

Literary Agents

Literary agents have emerged as the publishers' gatekeepers. They are middlemen and women, go-betweens, and facilitators. Approximately 80 percent of the books that publishing houses release were brought to them by agents.

Most publishing houses give agented submissions more attention because editors have a high level of confidence in agented submissions. They know that it's not in an agent's interest to waste their time. Agents won't waste editors' time because they have ongoing business relationships with editors that they don't want to jeopardize.

"An agent is effectively a vendor. He or she usually has already worked on the proposal, which gives me quality control and a partner in the creation of the book," Jeremy Katz, executive editor at Rodale, Inc., says. "The author isn't really my partner until I buy the book, but I'm in business with the agent."

Publishers rely on agents to screen submissions for several reasons:

- *Cost savings.* Since agents read manuscripts and proposals, publishers don't have to hire more screeners.
- *Selectivity.* Literary agents usually have experience, know quality, and know what sells. They usually won't try to interest publishers in stuff that's weak, except when it's written by a big celebrity.

■ *Insider knowledge.* Agents usually have a feel for the pulse of the industry. They are adept at spotting trends and usually know what's hot. Agents are often great talent spotters, and the good ones know what particular publishing companies and/or editors want and like.

On the flip side, publishers know that agents are commissioned salespeople and their livelihoods are directly tied to selling the books they pitch. Agents receive a commission, usually 15 percent, on whatever their writers receive. While publishers won't automatically sign every writer that agents recommend, they usually will read what agents' clients write.

Legally, agents represent authors; they are their client-writers' sales agents. When publishers pay authors for advances and royalties, they send checks to the agents, who deduct their fees and remit the balance to their clients. Since some agents tend to work with the same publishers or editors, they can become beholden to them. This can create delicate situations and agents must balance the interests of two, often conflicting, parties: authors and publishers.

An agent's primary job is to represent the writer and protect his or her interests. Much of this involves the selling of the book and negotiating the contract and fees. The work of a good agent continues long after the ink on the contract is dry. A good agent monitors the publisher's actions, sees that they are keeping their bargains and putting forth their best efforts to promote and distribute their clients' books. They also are watchful for future opportunities and push for follow-up books, additional printing runs, added publicity, and other benefits.

For most writers, getting a literary agent isn't easy. Agents don't make money unless they sell books, so they're selective about the clients they take on. Most agents simply can't afford to waste their time and energy on writers whose works won't sell. So increase your chances of getting an agent by understanding the process from the agent's perspective and following the protocols.

Publishers

Of the players in the publishing trinity, publishers hold the upper hand—they wield the most power. They occupy this position by virtue of the fact that they are willing to put up the money to finance the production of books and to distribute them.

In addition, publishers are the cornerstones of the book business; they are professionals, full-time players. Authors like you, on the other hand, are merely occasionally visitors, drop-ins. Publishers know all the industry rules and protocols. In fact, they wrote most of them. And in doing so, they sculpted them to their advantage. They created the rules on how the industry works.

Publishing professionals know all the industry players, the shortcuts, and the landmines. They are fluent in the industry language, which they also wrote. From the first moment you attempt to do business with publishers, you're operating on their turf and speaking in their language.

Publishers like to claim that they bear the largest financial risk in putting out a book, which they often do. However, many authors rightfully dispute this claim. Nevertheless, in publishing a book, publishers take on substantial financial risk because they must edit and prepare the book for publication, then print, market, and distribute it. Despite the technological breakthroughs, printing continues to be a big expense, as is distribution.

Besides being book financiers, publishing houses are also akin to book manufacturers because they take your work, refine it, print it, and bring it to market. As a result of their risk and involvement, they reserve the right to change your manuscript and package and promote it according to their expertise and vision. Frequently, their opinion of how your book should be edited, positioned, and promoted can conflict with that of the author and an adversarial relationship may result.

In such cases, agents should get involved to protect their authors and restore a good working relationship. However, some agents side with the publisher's position, which leaves authors feeling abandoned and betrayed. Frequently, when agents jump in and go to war, they don't have the clout to alter the publisher's decision.

In Praise of Publishers

Although publishers and authors often have conflicting objectives, they have many similar goals—the most significant being to produce the best and most widely read book. Publishers can be, and often are, writers' best friends. In addition to publishing writers' books, publishers can:

- Improve an author's writing, give it more impact and make it more readable, which can attract a larger and more influential audience.
- Sharpen the manuscript's focus by eliminating repetition and weak portions and suggesting new, more powerful additions and directions.
- Shape the marketing, promotional, and follow-up campaigns.
- Position the book with booksellers and book clubs and get it reviewed, excerpted, quoted, and serialized.
- Connect authors with career opportunities such as speaking and teaching engagements and may introduce authors to potential partners and sources of help.
- Sell subsidiary rights such as motion-picture rights, products, and marketing ventures.
- Suggest future titles, spin-offs, approaches, and families of books.

Self-Publishing

No discussion of the publishing industry would be complete without mentioning self-publishing. Over the last decade, technical breakthroughs have made self-publishing a viable alternative to traditional publishing. Instead of having to shop books to agents and publishing companies, writers can now create professional-quality books themselves.

Self-publishing is attractive to authors because it guarantees that their books will be published. By self-publishing, anyone can become a published author. Innovations such as print on demand (POD) and e-books have drastically decreased the initial self-publishing costs because authors no longer have to print and store substantial printing runs. In addition, they don't have to write query letters and proposals or deal with and pay agents. They, not publishing companies, get to keep the lion's share of the moneys their books make.

Authors who have self-published have subsequently sold their books to traditional publishers, and some have gone on to great success. Self-published books have also brought their authors' attention in their occupations and boosted their careers.

On the downside, self-publishing requires lots of work and has a high learning curve. Besides writing their books, self-published authors must learn about and take on many roles including those of a financer, editor, designer, book packager, schlepper, printer, distributor, fulfillment house, storage facilitator, promoter, marketer, and watchdog. Fortunately, they can contract out all or any of these functions and a number of experts have created businesses that now provide these services to self-publishers.

Unlike traditional publishing, in which authors receive advances against royalties upon signing with publishers, self-publishers must lay out a number of basic costs. Costs for editing, designing, printing, and promoting can be steep. Distribution can also be difficult because many booksellers don't stock, or limit their stocks of, self-published books.

Action Steps

1. Tell everyone you know you are writing a book. Say it out loud that you are going to become an author. Put it out in the universe.
2. Ask your family, friends, and contacts if they know anyone in the publishing business. From publishers to editors, publicists to authors, book designers to printers, and of course, literary agents. Anyone and everyone! Get the name and number of those individuals and

introduce yourself. Get to know someone who has been there and done that! Begin your author Rolodex. Think contacts, contacts, contacts.

3. Check out the books that relate to your topic of interest—fiction, nonfiction, children's books, etc. Begin noticing what publishers and imprints publish the genre of the book you wish to write. Start observing who publishes what!

4. Begin a list of publishers that seem suited to you. That's right! Make your list of which publishers might be an ideal match. What did they publish? Why are they suited to you? Which authors do what you want to do and what publisher did they team up with?

5. Get connected. Read everything you can about the authors whose careers you most admire and who write about the topic you are interested in. Attend their book signings, write them, visit their Web site.

Remember:

⚠ **Publishing is a business,** so understanding the publishing industry and how it works will increase your chances of getting your book published. Publishing is now dominated by six huge international corporations that put out 80 percent of the books published in the United States. If publishers think that your book won't make money, they probably won't publish it.

⚠ **Literary agents are publishers' gatekeepers.** They screen and represent the vast majority of the books publishers release. Publishing houses tend to give proposals submitted by agents more attention because their editors have a high level of confidence in their submissions. Don't approach agents or publishers before you complete the preliminary steps that will be detailed in the next chapter.

CHAPTER 2

"An aim in life is the only fortune worth finding. And it is not to be found in foreign lands, but in the heart itself."

Robert Louis Stevenson

Think Like a Published Author

THIS CHAPTER WILL COVER:

▶ What it takes
▶ Get in the pipeline
▶ What writers face
▶ Walk the walk—talk the talk

WHEN WRITERS TRY TO SELL THEIR BOOKS, they often feel like they're swimming against the tide in a tsunami. For most writers, the process of trying to sell a book differs from anything that they have ever attempted. For many, it's as if they're entering a strange new world, and they can quickly get lost or beaten down. When they are not fully prepared, they may suddenly discover that they have to do much more than they expected and do it in a manner that may not be their strength.

First-time writers are seldom prepared for the demands agents, editors, and publishers will ask them to satisfy in order to get published. Usually, they have no idea how to meet those requirements and find them surprisingly difficult and discouraging. Many get frustrated, disillusioned, and quit.

Often, just getting your foot in the door, having someone read your proposal or listen to your idea, can be daunting. But don't despair!

The good news is that every author at one time or another was a first-time author! Including us.

We know what it was like to want to land that first book deal. We understand where you are coming from and where you want to go. We, too, were once in your shoes and we know how it feels. On one hand, it's an exciting ride into the unknown that could end with your winning the lottery. However, on the other hand, it can be a frustrating waste of your time, effort, and money.

Before we take you through the details of how to write bestselling book proposals, it's essential that you have the right frame of mind. The proposal process can be brutal, so how you approach it can make the difference between whether you succeed or fail.

Get in the Pipeline

Virtually all published writers have had to invest an enormous cache of equity sweat. Then, they have had to adjust—to make compromises, change, or even give in. Great, top-selling books have taken complete U-turns from the projects that were initially proposed.

The publishing process is highly collaborative. Many voices are involved in publishing, and they often sing different tunes, many of which writers don't want to hear. However, it's the way the industry works.

So, if you want to get your book published, you must expect and learn to welcome input from the entire team. It isn't always easy, but it's absolutely mandatory! To see your book published, you may be asked to do and invest far more than you want and initially would have thought it was worth.

"Generally speaking, authors are ignorant about many essential parts of the publishing industry," agent Richard Curtis observes. "People who want to enter into the profession are finding the bar higher and higher and their options more limited. So my approach is to do whatever has to be done to get the author into the system so he or she has books to point to, sales numbers, and a Web site. The key is to get the author in the system because it's easier to work an author up than to break the author into the world of publishing."

It's all about the system. Ironically, many individuals become writers because they don't want to work within a system. They love the isolation of writing and the fact that they can work alone without a lot of interference. They don't want to become salespeople who are forced to promote their books. All they want is to write. As lone eagles they can chart their own courses, set their own goals, and answer only to themselves. So, it frequently comes as a shock to writers when they're asked to change, to take so much direction, and try to fit into the system in order to get their work published.

What Writers Face

When many writers begin thinking about getting their writing published, they're publishing novices. They have no knowledge or understanding of publishing, the overall system, and how it works. All they know, and care about, is that they want or need to write a book and get it published. They have no inkling of the demands they will face, and some don't care.

It looks glorious. It looks so glamorous. "Ah ... the life of an author," they think. They dream of book signings, television appearances, fans, accolades, and leading a celebrated life. They think it will be easy, but nothing about getting published is easy. It involves rewrites, rewrites, and more rewrites, plus critics, unappreciative readers, bad reviews, returns, cancelled publicity appearances, and more. Fun, fun, fun.

Believe us, when your book is published, the good times are fabulous and remarkably rewarding! But getting there requires an enormous amount of skill, time, and labor. And take it from us ... it ain't always glamorous!

Peter Applebome, the author of *Dixie Rising: How the South Is Shaping American Values, Politics, and Culture* and *Scout's Honor: A Father's Unlikely Foray into the Woods*, explains what it takes to get a publisher to put out your book: "I think there are three equally crucial parts of the proposal process. The first is doing a big chunk of the reporting and getting a sense, imperfect as it may be, of what's possible and what's not. The second is getting the voice right. The third and most important is thinking through who you're writing the book for and what you're trying to get across. It's one thing to have a vague sense in your mind. It's another to put down on paper what the book, at its heart, is about, and who's going to buy it and why."

According to Applebome, even after you get your proposal accepted and write your book, you've still only taken the first step to success. "I wish I knew how hard it is to sell a lot of books and how much you have to do yourself to make it happen," he continues. "Almost everyone I know thinks they're going to write a bestseller. Of course, almost no one does. Many absolutely brilliant books vanish without a trace. A fistful of great reviews don't guarantee you more than a spiffy Web site. So I wish I knew that writing a great book is only about a third of the game. The second third is what the publisher will do in terms of the printing and promotion. And the final third is how successful you are at ginning up every bit of good publicity and good marketing you can. Unless you're Tom Wolfe or John Grisham or lightning strikes, you need all three."

Most writers want to be published because they feel that they have something important to say. Frequently, these writers approach the publishing process naively. They think that all they have to do is write their book or transcribe their speeches or presentations and they will get a great book deal.

Then, when agents and publishers hit them with demands, they're blindsided, shocked, unprepared; they never imagined they would be required to do so much work. They see agents' and editors' submission requirements as unreasonable, as arbitrary constraints, unnecessary limits, and time-depleting restrictions that divert them from their true calling, purposes, or goal.

Others come into writing with long histories of successes. They have done it all, worked their way up from nothing, proven themselves, gained fame and fortune, and been lauded for their success. Usually, they're accustomed to leading, making the rules, setting the standards,

and calling the shots. So, it can be jarring when an agent or publisher insists that they write a detailed proposal, chapter summaries, analyze all similar books, and submit sample chapters—and to do so precisely in a rather unyielding format.

The protocol for becoming an author is clearly defined. The book proposal is your ticket to success. This is why we've devoted an entire book to it. As you begin your *Author 101* experience, we want to ease the process and help you get in the mind-set to succeed so you won't give up and let a good book go down the drain without an educated fight!

Walk the Walk

The rewards of getting your book published can be huge, but the costs can be steep. If you want to be a published writer, understand that you will probably have to adjust your thinking and walk the publisher's walk.

Your dynamic keynote speech that received that long standing ovation may not translate into a salable book; your comic routine that makes them double up in their seats may not work when it's put in writing. Your book that your children can't have read to them too often might not cut it in the competitive world of kids' books.

If you want to get your book published, you'll have to relearn how to walk. You'll have to learn how to walk the publishing walk, but when you do, you may be able to walk directly to the bank!

- Believe in your idea; keep that fire burning in your heart and stay convinced that your book must be published.
- Then feed agents, editors, and publishers exactly what they want. Play the game; walk the walk.

Walking the publishing walk is not simple; it's cluttered by many rules. Plus every house, editor, agent, bookseller, and reader has their own requirements, preferences and biases on what and how you must deliver.

Fortunately, each and every one of them is different. They have different backgrounds, different reactions, and different likes and dislikes. Also they can be open, curious, willing to take a chance, or like, understand, or identify with you. So follow their rules, as hard as they may seem, because it could get you noticed and increase your chances of selling your book.

Adopting a positive attitude is the hallmark of a professional, and it will pay off in the long run. Everyone—especially agents, editors, and publishers—wants to work with professionals; they ultimately will be

Robyn Says

"Years ago, I wrote a book called *The Thank You Book,* which has been revised, updated, and is still successfully in print and selling very well. That book embodied the spirit of my work as a writer. When I first shared the idea, I was told it was a magazine article, not a book. It would have been easy to quit right then and there, but I believed in the art of gratitude and knew this book was meant to be.

"I have put this book's philosophy to work throughout my career. If an editor assisted me, a librarian guided me or anyone offered me help or advice, I made an effort to send them a handwritten thank-you note. A key to success in any business is to express your appreciation to those individuals who make a difference in your career from the ground up! Keep in mind, an attitude of gratitude goes a long way!"

more accommodating and helpful to professionals. So, do yourself a big favor and make getting your book published easier by adjusting your outlook. Then, prepare to cash in.

Action Steps

1. Identify the items involved in getting your book published that you didn't expect. Just list the things that you can think of at this time without exploring further in this book.

2. List the items you must complete to get your book published that you don't feel comfortable with. What do you think your weaknesses will be? What haven't you ever done or don't do well?

3. List all of the possible benefits that getting your book published can bring. Think expansively. Don't just include those that should occur, but also list the wildest possibilities.

4. Compare the effort you will be required to make with the benefits that you might get. Will it be worth it?

5. Write what you think being a professional writer means to agents, editors, and publishers.

Remember:

⚠ **Aspiring writers are frequently not prepared for the obstacles they must overcome to get published.** For example, they may receive many conflicting opinions that they don't want to hear. Frequently, they don't know how to deal with them and find them difficult and discouraging. Many get frustrated and quit.

⚠ **If you want to get your book published, believe in your ideas.** Keep the fire burning in your heart, and remain dedicated and convinced that your book must be published. Give agents, editors, and publishers exactly what they want, even more than they ask. Play the game; walk the publishing walk. Develop a platform from which your voice can be clearly heard.

"Everywhere I go I'm asked if I think the university stifles writers. My opinion is that they don't stifle enough of them."
Flannery O'Connor

The Author's Platform

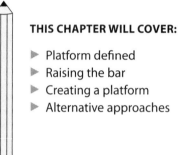

THIS CHAPTER WILL COVER:

▶ Platform defined
▶ Raising the bar
▶ Creating a platform
▶ Alternative approaches

OVER THE PAST DECADE, writers have been confronted with a substantial new barrier that is now keeping countless numbers of them from getting their nonfiction books published. It is the insistence by publishers that authors have what is known in the industry as a "national platform."

A platform means that the author has continuing national visibility. And many publishers have extended this demand to writers who have previously been published. Now, authors need more than good book ideas; they must be perceived by publishers as being entrepreneurial, promotion minded, and willing to aggressively market their books. To make those determinations, publishers look to author's platforms.

For business, psychology, parenting, and relationship books, a national platform is now virtually mandatory. Although exceptions do exist, publishers generally won't buy these types of books if the authors haven't firmly established themselves through speaking engagements, writing, media and Internet presence, a government post, a faculty position, and professional affiliations.

It's no longer enough to be an expert, even a published expert. To be published today, nonfiction authors must be experts who also have national platforms. Publishers want authors to be celebrities who are well known, admired, and have followers in their fields.

"It's a crowded marketplace," agent John Willig, president and founder of Literary Services, Inc., points out. "So publishers are looking for writers who write books that are aligned with the author's everyday work and practice. That alignment today is critical, plus the author must be involved in activities that can support the sales of the book's message, like speeches, workshops, and e-mail communities."

"It's not enough to just have the great idea or to have that great idea and be a great writer. Today, you also have to have a platform, which is a word taken from the IT world," Willig explains. "A platform translates to publishers as energy behind the book; it tells them that the author, the author's company, the author's e-mail community, and the author's following will help move the book in an extremely crowded marketplace."

Publishers tell us that authors must have platforms because it's hard to break out books—for them to become top sellers—when the authors don't have platforms. So they sign writers who have followings that will buy their books and who have proven that they have the ability and experience to vigorously promote their books. It's a way for publishers to hedge their bets.

According to publishing guru Michael Larsen, of San Francisco's Larsen-Pomada Literary Agents and the author of *How to Write a Book Proposal* (Writer's Digest Books, 3rd edition, 2004), "A platform is vital if an author (a) wants to be published by a big house and (b) the book is the type that requires author promotion. If an author has enough promotional ammunition, they or their agent can approach big houses right away."

A number of agents and editors informed us that the need for a platform has filtered through the publishing chain. Second- and third-tier publishers and even small, specialty houses are now demanding platforms.

"Now, bright young people who write well, but don't have wide and clever ways to promote themselves, often get passed over," agent and book packager John Monteleone, of Mountain Lion, Inc., laments. "They don't have the promotional end down. Publishers don't just want to stock the book in the warehouse; they want to get it sold. They will always publish someone who can get books sold ahead of someone who can write a good book."

Some smaller publishers are not as platform focused, but an author's platform still carries weight. "We do very well with first-time authors and like to help them build track records," Acquisitions Editor Danielle Chiotti of Adams Media (the publisher of this book) discloses. "At Adams, the platform is not as important, but it helps. If an author already has a strong platform, it's tremendously helpful and can sway a decision. It makes the job of the publicity and marketing people easier when I bring them an author who has a good platform. If we love a concept and what the author brings to the table, we would not turn him or her away because he or she doesn't have a platform; we would find a way to make it work."

Platforms Are Essential

Not so long ago, publishers didn't insist that writers have platforms. If a good writer also had a platform, it was great. The platform was considered a bonus, something extra that the writer could contribute.

"Say you're a woman who spent her entire life raising kids, owned a very successful day-care center or was a foster mom, who had successfully raised many children, her own and those she took," June Clark, a New York agent with the Peter Rubie Literary Agency Ltd., says. "If she wanted to write a parenting book, they would look at her and say, 'You don't have a platform.' It wasn't like that years ago. Now, you have to be a nurse, a pediatrician, a child psychologist, and have a following.

A couple of people have snuck under that wire who were witty writers or journalists with contacts, but it's very, very difficult," Clark declares.

In the past, authors could just be authors. However, the success of books by authors with platforms poisoned the well for other writers. Now, authors must have platforms. And not only is the platform a requirement, but the bar for that requirement is continually being raised.

Roger Cooper, executive vice president of I Books, Inc., puts it best: "The level of the platform keeps increasing. It used to be that you could have a column in a regional newspaper and go on a couple of radio shows. Then it became more national syndication, then the *Today Show* or *Dateline*, and then *Oprah* or *Dr. Phil*. The bar keeps on being raised by publishers who, more and more, want authors who have higher platforms. It used to be a silver platform, then it became a gold platform and now it's a platinum platform."

"It's almost as if the marketing people want the book to sell without their doing a lot so they therefore rationalize the money that is spent on the book as an advance," Cooper adds. "It shows a lack of creative energy in making something happen on the publishers' side. Even if you have a medical book by a doctor who is brilliant and incredibly well credentialed on a subject that is very provocative and salable, if that doctor doesn't have a platform, you have a diminished chance of selling that book."

"The bar for platforms has been raised to almost absurd heights," according to agent Sharlene Martin, of Martin Literary Management in Encino, California. "A whole plethora of good writing is being ignored because it doesn't have the promotional hooks that publishers are now demanding. If you have a book on woodworking, you better be a contributor to a woodworking magazine, have appeared on shows about woodworking, give seminars on it, speak about it all the time, have your own newsletter and Web site."

Agent Richard Curtis offers an encouraging note. "The bar in publishing has been raised extremely high, but not impossibly high," he says. "A good book will still rise to the surface if it's a really good book."

And don't forget lucky breaks! Sometimes endorsements from famous authors, experts, or celebrities help position a book. It's not just what you know, but who you know. Your book has to be a quality book, but it doesn't hurt to be validated by respected sources who think you have something important to say.

Certain rare and special ideas can transcend the platform requirement. These books touch a particular nerve, involve innovative theories or capture the public's heart. Examples of these qualities are the *Chicken Soup for the Soul* series of books (Health Communications, Inc.) and *The Tipping Point* by Malcolm Gladwell (Little, Brown and Company, 2000).

Creating a Platform

Since a platform has taken on such importance, agents and publishers find themselves advising promising writers to go back, build a platform and them come back and see them.

"If someone doesn't have a platform, I usually tell them that they are before their time," agent Sharlene Martin says. "They are too young, too fresh, they need to spend the next couple of years getting a Web site up, doing public speaking, and publishing articles. Volunteer to become an expert by getting yourself in some expert directories and then you'll be ready."

According to publishing expert Michael Larsen, the main ways to build a platform are by:

1. *Giving talks around the country* (the most common method). However, "It can be a Catch-22," agent Bonnie Solow, of Solow Literary Enterprises in Santa Monica, notes. "Writers often can't get speaking engagements without a book and they can't get a book without a platform."

   Time is the big problem. You can't just pick up the phone or make a wish and, presto, you're on *Oprah*. You have to build incrementally, step-by-step. Start small and locally; approach civic, community, and religious organizations. Develop a series of talks for the Y, your church, or the Rotary Club and then move up.

Talk to everyone you know, network, beat the bushes. Find places to start, get bookings and work your way up. Make your initial mistakes locally and build a devoted following close to home. Take speaking, voice, or acting lessons, or hire a media coach. Join Toastmasters and the National Speakers Association. Tape your performances; critique them; and practice, practice, practice.

2. *Gaining media presence.* Write a regularly published column, newsletter, or blog with significant national exposure; become the expert whom reporters interview on your area of expertise; and regularly appear on television or cable.

3. *Using the Internet.* Build a following as the leader of or an active participant in Internet communities that focus on the subject matter of the book.

4. *Enlisting support for the book from one or more noncompeting promotional partners.* An example is getting a business or nonprofit organization that is excited enough about the book to write a letter that can be added at the end of the proposal. The letter must commit to buying copies of the book, sending the author on a national promotional tour, or featuring the author in the organization's advertising or on its Web site and internal media.

"Identify your following, your power base. Find out who they are, what they have in common, and what attracts them to you. Then come up with ways to constantly massage your following, to keep in contact with them and give them something they can use.

Create an enormous e-mail list, a newsletter that people want to read and a great Web site. Run discussion groups and infomercials; provide products or services that get you continual media coverage. Get others to believe in your cause and come under your wing. Find ways to get input from your following so that you can give them what they want, and to enable your following to grow."

Merely pointing out the possibility of getting promotional partners in a proposal will not be convincing. "Without a letter, a promotional partner is only an idea. Publishers want commitments," Larsen stresses.

Additional ways to build a platform include:

- *Publishing your chapters.* Build publishing credentials by submitting your sample chapters as articles to magazines, newsletters, or journals. Being a published author will help you attract agents and publishers as well as overcome the lack of or a weak platform.

- *Developing a great Web site.* "We are moving into a visually, graphically active, interactive world through the Internet, television, games, cell phones, and Amazon," agent Richard Curtis explains. "When I pitch authors to editors over the phone, I can actually hear them typing on the keyboard as we speak. I know that while we're talking, they are going on Google or Amazon and checking out the author. They'll say, 'Oh yeah, I see the author's picture or the cover of his last five books.' So, if that's what editors now do in order to identify a writer and place him or her in a context that they feel comfortable with, let's give it to them."

  The trick, according to Curtis, is to create a presence or the appearance of a platform that editors can easily find and with which they can relate. So he starts by working with authors to create impressive Web sites, which he believes are imperative for authors in today's interactive world.

- *Creating a qualitative survey.* Conduct surveys to test, support, or document the central theory in your book. Hire a company that specializes in running surveys or do it yourself. A survey can demonstrate the need for your book. Running the first survey on a subject or an aspect of it can establish you as an authority on that subject; it will make both you and your survey newsworthy. You will attract media coverage because the media love to report on surveys. If a survey demonstrates a need for your book, you will be more likely to sell it.

■ *Conducting focus groups.* Focus groups that test your book or its concepts can add credibility and help you build your platform in several ways. For example:

   a. The information focus groups provide can show you ways to strengthen your book.

   b. The answers you receive can boost your stature in your field.

   c. When eighteen of twenty group members say that they benefited from your program, information, or advice, they become a part of your following, and their testimonials can add weight to your platform.

■ *Documenting your success.* Build your expertise, legitimacy, and following with illustrations of your approaches' success. Take before and after photographs to submit with your proposal for your weight-loss book, or diary entries that show that your methods work and the clear benefit they provide.

■ *Compiling a names list.* Compile a list of people who would be interested in buying your book. Check if similar lists are available through list brokers and investigate the value of purchasing them. Publishers like names lists because they help them target book promotions and they also identify a segment of your potential following.

How writers present themselves and the information they provide on their sites can be revealing for agents and editors. Since we're living in an increasingly electronic world, editors can refer others in the acquisition process to a writer's Web site for information that may impact the decision on whether or not to buy a book.

In this electronic age, having a top-notch Web site shows that a writer is professional. Increasingly, editors are viewing them as tickets to the game.

If you're a nonfiction author and you have a body of knowledge, it's very important to have a Web site even if it doesn't reach that many people. The Web site is another piece of the marketing puzzle because it gives you a presence in the market in the eyes of publishers. It helps an editor to sell your proposal when you have a robust Web site, Q & As, a chat room about your topic, and your own newsletter going out to 2,500 people. Authors should also agree to link their Web sites with other reference sites to help the consumer get information. That makes the author more of an expert and makes his or her site a place for browsers to go.

Before you continue reading, ask yourself these questions:

- What is your platform?
- What makes you unique; how do you stand out?
- Who are your followers who will spread your message?
- Where can you go to deliver your message?
- Will people buy a book about your message?

Alternative Approaches

If you are having trouble getting published because of a lack of a national platform, consider some of the following options. As you examine these alternatives, try to think out of the box, to creatively convince agents, editors, and publishers to give you a shot. Some of your options are:

- *Writing humorously.* If you're funny and can write witty, humorous books, you stand a good chance of being immunized from the platform requirement. Publishers are always looking for lively, fun-filled books and are usually open to publishing authors, even first-time authors, who don't have a platform, but can make readers laugh.
- *Plugging into an established book series.* If a series covers important subjects and has established a brand name, it's built a following. Good examples are the *Dummies, Chicken Soup, Everything,* and *Streetwise* book series. With series, the brand and reputation are what sell and are more important than the writer's platform.

Publishers can plug good writers who do not have national platforms into these series, but the writers still need credentials, even if they don't need big, impressive platforms.

■ *Being recommended by a great agent.* Publishing is a relationship and reputation business. Some literary agents have such great reputations and wonderful relationships with editors that the editors will read anything the agents recommend. When they truly believe in a writer, they may put their reputation and relationship on the line by recommending an unplatformed writer's proposal. New Haven agent Don Gastwirth, of Don Gastwirth & Associates, will state in his cover letter, "This is really important to me and I think it should be important to you." "However," he cautions, "they will only read it once. So, it better be good because you are only as good as your last submission."

■ *Hiring book publicists.* Authors who are willing to hire publicists who specialize in promoting books can neutralize some of the fallout from the fact that they don't have national platforms. Publishers are familiar with publicists and how they can boost book sales. Any publicist you hire must be highly regarded by publishers and must, as part of the promotional campaign, build the author's platform.

Turn to Smaller or Niche Publishers

Although the platform requirement has penetrated all levels of publishing, some smaller and niche publishers remain committed to putting out quality books on their subjects. Many of these publishers will take on authors who lack platforms. Attend BookExpo America, the huge annual national book trade show, and see small houses and presses—thousands of them exist. Speak with them, look at their publications and their lists to see if any of them could be a good match for you. For many writers, it's better to be an important, prized author with a small publisher than to be a small, neglected author at a big publishing house.

"When buyers are looking at books on the shelves, they're going to buy the one that seems the most authoritative for the price they're willing to pay," book packager Leanne Chearney of Amaranth declares. "Although the platform requirement has filtered down to smaller publishers, it's still more important to the large publishers; in fact, it's basically required. The only books big publishers want are books that can be blockbusters, books that they think they can break out on the bestseller list. And they don't think they can do that unless the author has a great platform. If you don't need your book to be a blockbuster or if you don't have a great platform, try sending your proposal to smaller publishers that don't place such emphasis on the bestseller list," Chearney advises.

Think Locally!

Local and regional publishers can present great opportunities for writers. Often, the most important objective should be getting published, getting that initial notch in your belt, being able to say that you are a published author.

Small and regional presses can provide you with opportunities to display your writing talent. Look into the local and regional presses in your area, learn what kind of books they publish, and visit and speak with their staffs. Although they may not publish many books, they may be interested in publishing yours because you live locally. Many small presses are dedicated to writing and writers and are eager to help authors learn their trade and start their careers.

Join Forces with Professionals

When some editors receive excellent submissions from writers who have no platforms, they may try to pair them with people who have credentials and/or followings. For example, if an author who wrote a diet book doesn't have a degree in nutrition, they may try to connect him or her with a doctor or a nutritionist. Unfortunately, egos, disputes regarding responsibilities, and other problems sometimes waylay these projects. Also, authors with platforms may resist because they don't see the need for a collaborator or they may try to diminish the cowriter's role.

Pairings seem to work best when authors are matched before the actual writing begins. Then they can plan the book together, divide responsibilities, and decide how they will work. Even so, coauthoring can be a difficult and taxing experience. On the positive side, Robyn offers this account of a successful collaboration:

> I'll never forget when I wanted to write a book to inspire other moms on ways to creatively encourage positive behavior in their kids. I certainly didn't know a great deal about the psychology of human behavior, but I was a former teacher and a new mom who was challenged with a busy child. After I wrote a book on entertaining kids, my agent arranged for me to meet an editor during a trip to New York. This editor said, "Your ideas are really creative, but if you teamed up with seasoned professionals, you just might have something really marketable." So, I called up Drs. Stephen and Marianne Garber, a well-known child psychologist and his wife/partner, who was a highly regarded educational consultant, and they, too, had wanted to write a book on behavior. We assembled a focus group of parents to determine what their kids were doing that concerned and drove them crazy. And the book proposal was on its way. We ended up with a list of over 100 problem behaviors, from spitting, hitting, and fighting to refusing to go to sleep and take no for an answer! That effort resulted in the book *Good Behavior: Over 1,200 Sensible Solutions to Your Child's Problems from Birth to Age Twelve* (Villard/Random House, 1987).
>
> While I didn't have a Ph.D., I appeared weekly as Super Mom for my clever ideas on the local *Noonday* talk show on NBC in Atlanta and created a following for my how-to tips. However, I was also a real mom who tested the ideas in the book and gained a tremendous amount of knowledge from the Garbers. My voice was that I was in the trenches and brought my creative spin to the application of our ideas.

Alternative Forms of Writing and Publishing

Many authors who cannot get their books published by traditional houses are turning to self-publishing and putting out e-books. Increasingly, traditional publishers are monitoring self-publishing and e-book offerings and buying those that show promise for their lists. Authors of self-published and e-books have taken booths at BookExpo America, which gives them wide exposure to publishers who may be hunting for new properties. Many of these publishers find out about nontraditionally published books by reading reviews on *authorlink.com* and *bookreporter.com*.

When authors pay to have their books published, it's called vanity publishing. Some vanity publishers may design the covers and get involved in distribution and publicity, but mainly they just print the books. According to most publishing professionals, they don't do a very good job.

Another option is ghost writing. Writers tend to fall into two general categories: (1) those whose main objective is to pursue writing careers and (2) those who want to write to further their careers. If you're in category 1, you can build your writing career by writing with or for someone in category 2. When you publish the book, you will be credited as a published writer, which is an important step in building a platform. Being a published author opens many doors. Showing agents and editors that your book has been published will increase their confidence that if they take on your project, you will deliver.

Action Steps

1. *Define your platform.* Once your message is clear, you can address how you will share it with others. What is your platform? Be clear about how your message will benefit others and what makes it helpful, inspirational, entertaining, and unique.
2. *Start with one!* Make a list of all the community organizations you belong to—your religious affiliation, local garden clubs, civic

organizations, and so forth—and get booked with a speech. Even if you start with just one group, eventually you can branch out and approach others.

3. *Align with a media outlet that reaches your desired audience and write how-to articles or short stories for them.* Share your platform. The most comfortable for most people is print, so develop any opportunity that will give you space!

4. *Work your way up to newspaper and magazine print interviews, local radio talk shows, and television appearances.* Keep a tape or request a copy of each and every appearance. Have your best tapes consolidated.

5. *Keep records of your appearances and document what you've done.* This will be especially helpful when writing your bio and demonstrating your promotional abilities.

Remember:

⚠ **Most publishers now require nonfiction writers to have national platforms.** This means that they have continuing national visibility. Publishers want authors who are entrepreneurial, promotion minded, and willing to aggressively market their books.

⚠ **Create a national platform by giving talks, speeches, and participating in workshops.** Write columns and articles and become a frequent interview subject. Develop a dynamic Web site, make strategic alliances, and link to the sites of those with whom you are aligned, and build an extensive list of names. Increase your visibility and your brand. Then understand the steps that are involved in the publishing process.

CHAPTER 4

"Before anything else, preparation is the key to success."
Alexander Graham Bell

Preliminary Steps

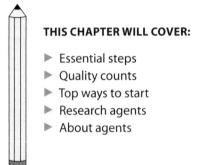

THIS CHAPTER WILL COVER:

▶ Essential steps
▶ Quality counts
▶ Top ways to start
▶ Research agents
▶ About agents

BEFORE YOU WRITE a book proposal, a number of preliminary steps must be completed or agents and publishers probably won't give it much consideration. These steps include developing a strong book concept, an interesting approach and a catchy title. You must also clearly identify your market and your niche and understand the purpose of your book proposal.

Think of these preliminary steps as laying the groundwork that will increase the chances of your writing a better book and getting it published. We assume that by now you have taken those steps, but just to be on the safe side, let's briefly review them.

Step #1: Have a Strong Book Concept

It all starts with the idea. If you want a publisher to buy your book, it must be on a subject or subjects that a publisher believes readers need or want to read. Readers have virtually endless options. According to book-marketing guru Dan Poynter (*http://parapublishing.com/statistics*), consumers purchased 1.6 billion books in 2001. That's a lot of books and a lot of competition! Since authors vie for a limited pool of readers' dollars, the concept of the book you propose must be strong enough to convince agents and editors that you have an idea for a book that consumers will pay to read. You may have the most fascinating idea or insight, you may write like John Updike or Joyce Carol Oates, but if you don't write what readers want or need to read, publishers usually won't buy.

Many good ideas simply don't work or translate in book form. For example, the crowd-pleasing speeches you've delivered for years may put readers to sleep when they're reduced to print. Some great ideas may make wonderful magazine articles but are not meaty or interesting enough to be stretched into entire books. Or your ideas, however intriguing, may be too complex, theoretical, impractical, or unrealistic. They may have been already done to death, may not address a sufficient audience, or may be just too boring when they run for more than ten pages.

Award-winning journalist Guy Garcia, author of *The New Mainstream: How the Multicultural Consumer Is Transforming American Business* (Rayo, HarperCollins Publishers, 2004), tells writers, "Don't rely on anyone for anything when it comes to getting your book published. Your editor will edit you and your agent will help close the deal. However, you must be involved at every step of the way and be informed. Your involvement begins at the proposal/outline stage. Test your idea on a few trusted readers, but most of all test it on yourself: Are you excited by the concept? If you could write anything, is this what it would be?"

"Books are artifacts of a personal journey," Garcia continues, "a journey in which the reader joins the writer. Your own excitement and sense of discovery will spill over onto the page and pull the reader along with you. Don't be afraid to stretch and reach for something that inspires you; the burning urge to get your thoughts on paper, to bring your ideas to life through language, is what will sustain you through the long solitary hours of getting a book done."

Step #2: Discover an Interesting Approach

Few books contain completely new topics or information. Most of what is written has been written before in one form or another. Books frequently build on and develop what has been previously written. Unless you supply completely new ideas or information, you must present your material differently, in a way that readers haven't read before. Although you don't have to reinvent the wheel, your book must have characteristics that distinguish it from its competitors; it must take some new or innovative approach that will appeal to both publishers and readers. Your new approach could be a novel point of view, new ideas or information, or simply a different format or way of stating your case. It could be a graphic representation of something that has been previously done in narrative form or vice versa. If you present the same old thing and take the same old approach, it probably won't sell, even if your writing is fabulous.

Step #3: Create a Great Title

Never underestimate the power of titles. We live in a society in which people respond to headlines, sound bites, short blasts of information that tell them all they need to know in the shortest amount of time. Since most of us are constantly surrounded by voices competing for our attention, we actually take the time to truly listen to only those things that somehow blast through the noise and clutter. Terrific titles penetrate our defenses and capture our attention. They make browsers stop, pick up books, and examine them more closely to learn what they're about. Fabulous titles sell books. Many books are bought simply because of their titles.

A title should be memorable, elicit a strong reaction or response, and create immediate interest. A wonderful title doesn't have to clearly communicate what the book is about, although that helps. It does, however, have to attract interest. Without a good title, the brilliance of your concept, writing, or format may be lost because no one will be interested or take that extra step to find out what your book is about.

If you have a great title but its meaning isn't completely clear, follow it up with a descriptive subtitle that tells the reader exactly what the book is about. The best titles usually run no more than five or six words, but subtitles can be double that amount. In most cases, the point of a subtitle is not to be witty or clever, but to clarify what your book is about and the benefits it will provide to readers.

"One proposal that grabbed me was Sam Horn's *Tongue Fu: How to Deflect, Disarm, and Defuse Any Verbal Conflict*," Jennifer Enderlin, Associate Publisher at St. Martin's Press, reports. "First, I loved the title. This is a book about verbal self-defense, and the title captured that in a vivid, imaginative way. Then, the author clearly outlined what she was going to accomplish in her book. She then took the time to research competing books, and explain how and why hers was different. Finally, she included sample chapters that showed how some of her techniques worked."

Step #4: Clearly Identify the Market

Since publishing is a business, the book you propose must be directed at a definable audience. Clearly tell publishers or agents the exact demographic group or groups that will buy your book so that they can estimate your book's sales potential. Try to quantify the size of your potential market. How many people are in the group that you're writing for? Understand that the size of the potential market for your book will vary according to your book's nature. For example, the market for a poetry book will differ from that of a title recalling lurid Hollywood scandals. In turn, the nature of your book will influence your decision as to which agents and publishers you approach. We will discuss the market for your book in greater detail in Chapter 11.

Step #5: Conduct Research

When agents and publishers consider books, one of the first questions they ask is "How does it compare to other books on the subject?" So you must be able to distinguish it from the other books in the market. If you advertise yourself as an expert on your subject, it's your job to know everything that has been published in your field. Reading others will also help you get additional ideas and information to develop and distinguish your own ideas. Identify how your book differs from other books on the subject and specifically note how they treat your central themes. Find your niche by discovering how your book differs, where it is stronger, weaker, or better. Is it clearer, more up to date, or better researched? Does it plow the same ground as other books, but addresses a different or perhaps larger audience or has a different format? Knowing this information is essential, especially when you try to sell your book to agents or editors.

Step #6: Market Your Idea to Agents and/or Editors

To sort through the tons of inquiries they receive about books, agents and publishing companies have devised a procedure. First, they require aspiring authors to send them query letters or e-mails describing their projects. We discuss query letters in detail in Chapter 6. If, after reading the queries, the agents or editors are interested, they request that the authors submit book proposals that follow the formats that we will outline in this book. At this stage of the game, book proposals are marketing documents that are intended to convince agents and publishers to take on the authors' books. To do so, they must follow the formats and contain the ingredients set forth in this book.

"To become an author, you have to have first a passion for your work and then let that passion drive your thoughts and innovative ideas into the world you live in," Stedman Graham, author of *Move Without the Ball: Put Your Skills and Your Magic to Work for You* (Fireside, 2004), advises. "You must be able to share your message or story and once you have that idea in place, the second part is how do you deliver that and who can you interest in the idea?"

"It's all in the planning and preparation, and demands writing a book proposal that's well thought out. The most important thing to do in your proposal is to figure out why people would want to buy this book and realize the publisher is in the business to sell books and fill a need in the marketplace. You're the middle person between the publisher and the consumer."

Ten Questions to Ask Yourself

Besides following the above steps, every writer should answer the following ten questions before starting to write a book. They are:

1. Why do I want to write this book?
2. Am I writing it for fame or fortune?
3. Can I afford to give my time to this book, even if I don't succeed?
4. What am I willing to invest in this project?
5. Should I team up with someone to help me with this book?
6. Am I a competent writer, or do I need to brush up on the basics and take a writing course?
7. Do I know anyone whom I can call to see what writing a book is really like? If not, do I have the guts to cold call?
8. If this book is published, what am I going to do to help make it a success?
9. Who will come to my book signing and support me if I write this book?
10. If I write a book proposal and no one buys this book, will my investment of time still be worthwhile?

Quality Counts

While it's not our intention to teach you how to write, we want to stress how essential it is for you to write a top-quality book. To interest agents and publishers, your book must be interesting and well written and must benefit readers by giving them lots of information that they need.

Writing a high-quality book is important for many reasons:

1. *Your name will be on it.* Books are permanent and can outlive you. Your books will represent you during your life and will impact your family long after you're gone. Your name and your books will always be linked in the public's mind as well as in the records at

the U.S. Copyright Office, in online search engines, and in libraries throughout the world.

2. *In most cases, books must be good to be published and to sell.* Sure, celebrity tell-alls, bodice rippers, and absolute clunkers always slip through, but by and large, they're exceptions. As a rule, publishers want books that contain good information, are well written, and will sell; they look for quality.

3. *Agents and publishers seek authors who can build long writing careers.* They prefer them to one-shot wonders who turn out just one hit book. For agents and publishers, good, prolific writers become annuities; dependable cash producers that they can count on and take to the bank. As a result, they will take a more active and nurturing role in developing promising writers' careers.

4. *A writer's name and reputation are his or her brand.* If writers are successful and are acknowledged to consistently produce good books, agents and publishers will vie to represent them and want all their new work. However, if they produce inferior work or don't deliver as promised, they will alienate their supporters.

Plenty of terrific books exist that can teach you about writing and help you to create a quality book. If you're not clear on what that takes, read some of them before you go any further.

Before you submit your writing to an agent or publisher, consider having it reviewed by a professional editor. It could be well worth the investment! Editors can shape up your writing and make it glitter. Agents are put off by poorly written, grammatically incorrect submissions and may not waste much of their time on them. Those who continue and see some promise in your book may recommend that you work with a professional editor. To make the best initial impression, have it edited before you submit it.

Reinvent Yourself

If you've written before, don't be afraid to reinvent yourself or try writing differently. Everything has a life cycle, and what you're doing, no matter how successful, can grow old. Build aggressively on your success by constantly doing and giving more. Don't hesitate to experiment or be bold.

Besides giving your following something new and invigorating, reinvention stimulates writers and keeps their work exciting and fresh. Regardless of your success or lack of success, writers must continue to search for that new idea, that breakthrough that can catapult them to the next level. Look at the examples of some of Rick's best-known, bestselling clients.

Although the *Chicken Soup* books brought Jack Canfield and Mark Victor Hansen overwhelming success, they both reinvented themselves: Mark with his book *The One Minute Millionaire* (coauthored by Robert G. Allen, Harmony, 2002), and Jack with *The Success Principles* (coauthored by Jane Switzer, HarperResource, 2004).

Harvey Mackay had a formula that kept him on the bestseller lists, but in his new book, *We Got Fired! . . . And It's the Best Thing That Ever Happened to Us* (Ballantine Books, 2004), he decided to take a new and successful approach. Although Robert Kiyosaki's books may look like they follow the same path that has made them so popular, each new title adds more: a new twist, a different emphasis, or additional information.

Top Ways to Start

If, like most people, you don't personally know agents or publishers, here's how to start. Get your writing career in gear by taking the following steps:

Step #1: Network

Turn to your family, friends, coworkers, and network members to get names. Personal introductions are often the most effective way of getting an agent or publisher's ear.

- Contact everyone you know to obtain introductions; leave no stone unturned.
- Question each person you meet and with whom you deal; he or she just may be able to help.
- Ask people you meet if they know agents or publishers or know others who might.

In most cases, those with publishing contacts will happily assist you. In fact, you may be surprised by how helpful and even generous they will be. They understand how difficult it is to get published and usually enjoy helping worthy colleagues. Many would love to play a part in your success.

If you find people with publishing contacts, ask them to introduce you. Try to get them to make a personal call on your behalf, but settle for a note or an e-mail—whatever can get your foot in the door.

Help your contacts by sending them a half-page summary of your book. Bullet the five or six most important features and include a two- or three-sentence biography of yourself that stresses why you're so qualified to write this book.

Step #2: Contact Teachers

Approach your present and former teachers, instructors, and professors; many of them have publishing contacts. Frequently, they, their colleagues and former students have been published and they can give you great leads. Your teachers know the quality of your work, so they can give you a strong recommendation. Plus, their introductions usually carry weight.

Step #3: Approach Bookstores and Libraries

Speak with staff members at your local bookstores and libraries. Many bookstores hold author events such as book signings and discussion groups. Their staff members may be writers or literary groupies and have great connections.

"Publishers and agents are professionals, books are their business, and they're always on the hunt for great writers and books; they don't want mediocre books.

"Remember, these are seasoned experts who are excellent judges of content and quality. Writers should fall in love with their ideas; however, you have to separate from the book and really ask yourself, if you glanced at this book:

> Would you buy it?
> What benefit does it provide the reader?
> When you reread it, is it really all that fabulous?
> If it's fiction, is it really a page-turner?
> Do unbiased individuals who read a great deal or have a literary background really think it's all that amazing?

"Writing an outstanding book will dramatically increase the prospects of its being published and of agents and publishers taking a more supportive role in your career. So hone your craft and get it right before you try to market your book."

Librarians tend to be dedicated to reading, information, and books. They routinely help local authors and may have developed personal relationships with them. Usually, they will be glad to help.

Step #4: Get to Know Published Authors

Meet published writers and network. Some ways you can do this include:

- Going to book signings and events where writers speak or are in attendance.
- Joining organizations like your local writers association and the Authors Guild and attend functions that they present.

- Participating in online chat groups.
- Taking writing and publishing courses at your local college or outreach center.
- Meeting people who are interested in writing and publishing and learn, learn, learn.

Pursue even the most remote connections, including anyone in any facet of the book and publishing business. Someone who works in a publisher's accounting department may know a designer who can connect you with an editor. Work your way up the ladder, step by step, because each rung could bring you closer to your ultimate targets and lead you to better, more helpful contacts.

Step #5: Speak with Avid Readers

Devoted readers frequently know writers and publishing professionals; they tend to read about writers and follow the publishing industry. They may be able to give you valuable information and leads.

Step #6: Explore Leads

Follow every lead and try to zero in on people who can help. When you identify targets, learn everything about them before you approach them, such as their backgrounds, education, past experiences, achievements, and hobbies. Look for common links or similar backgrounds, interests, or experiences. Then work backward and see if you can connect any of their experiences or interests to people you know or can reach.

Step #7: Be Patient and Appreciative

Understand that the process of making solid connections with people who can help you could take some time. When others help make your dreams come true, thank them. Send them a written note, and when your book is published, express your appreciation in the acknowledgment section and by sending them a copy in which you thank them again.

Research Agents

Leaf through books that are similar to yours to find the names of agents and editors. Search bookstores, libraries, and online booksellers. If you can't find other publications directly on point or somewhat close, broaden your search to see who wrote and published books on the same or related subjects.

When you find similar books, read the acknowledgments to find whom the authors thanked. Authors usually state their appreciation of their editors and agents in their books' acknowledgment section. Conduct additional research on those editors and agents.

A number of guidebooks and online guides exist to help you obtain information about agents. They usually provide the agent's contact information, areas of specialty, and additional information. Some of these are:

- *Guide to Book Publishers, Editors & Literary Agents*, by Jeff Herman (The Writer Books, published annually)
- *The Writer's Market*, by Kathryn S. Brogan and Robert Lee Brewer (Writer's Digest Books, published annually)
- *The Literary Market Place: The Directory of the American Book Publishing Industry with Industry Yellow Pages* (Information Today, Inc., published annually)
- *Literary Agents: What They Do, How They Do It, and How to Find and Work with the Right One for You*, by Michael Larsen (Wiley, 1996)
- *Everyone Who's Anyone in Adult Trade Publishing and Tinseltown Too*, by Gerard Jones, searchable online directory at *http://everyonewhosanyone.com*.

"If a writer has no clue of what agent to approach, the guidebooks won't offer much initial help," Santa Monica agent Bonnie Solow reveals. "Go to the bookshelf and find books that you consider kindred spirits. Typically, authors will have acknowledged their agents in their books. Then research them."

Go to the guidebooks and to the publishers' and agents' Web sites. See if they accept unsolicited submissions. Submission requirements are usually posted in the "Author" or "Contact Us" sections of publishers' Web sites. Note their specialty areas and the types of properties they accept. If they could be right for you, verify all contact information and carefully record the correct spelling of those you plan to contact.

The reference guidebooks mentioned above are published annually. So make sure to use only the current edition because people in the publishing business frequently move and these guidebooks can be out of date. Be especially wary of the volumes in local libraries because they are often several years old.

Additional options for finding names are to call literary agencies and publishing companies. Ask (1) who was the editor or agent on a similar book, or (2) who handles books on your particular topic. If you come up with names, double check the spelling and get the exact address where they can be contacted. Then, verify all the information you obtained in the reference guidebooks and Web sites.

Compile a list of potential publishers and/or agents to contact. Before you submit a proposal or a query letter, learn what kinds of books they handle, and how they wish to receive submissions. Note the information you obtain on a contact list as follows:

AGENT CONTACT LIST

Name and Firm	Specialties	Contact Information	Submission Requirements
Jeffrey Long, The Literary Group	Fiction, memoirs, short stories	xxxx@x.com 555-555-1161	Postal query letter, first 15 manuscript pages, SASE
Marjie Turell, The Mema Agency	Art and design	xxxx@x.com 555-555-5151	Query letter, samples of art
Doug Devon, Creative Literary	Mystery, science fiction, suspense	xxxx@x.com 555-555-4567	Query letter, excellent credentials, bio, SASE
Marcy O'Dawd, O'Dawd Agency	Children's books	xxxx@x.com 555-555-2121	Query letter, sample chapter, sample illustrations

Keeping a contact list will help you give publishers and agents exactly what they require in the precise format they want. It will also form the basis for a log on which you should track the submissions you send. Your submission log should include (1) the names of those you sent submissions to, (2) the date they were sent, (3) the responses you received, and (4) any follow-up requirements.

SUBMISSION LOG

Name	Firm	Date Sent	Response	Follow Up
Jeffrey Long	The Literary Group	11/17/05	Send proposal	Sent 1/7/06
Marjie Turell	The Mema Agency	11/17/05	Not interested	
Doug Devon	Creative Literary	11/20/05	Wants exclusive	Decide & contact by 1/10/06
Don Dontalone	Big Books	11/20/05	No response	

As we've noted, many publishers and agents do not accept unsolicited submissions, including query letters. However, those that do, usually provide clear submission guidelines on their sites. If they do accept unsolicited materials, identify exactly what they want, the format they prefer, and the address where your submission should be sent.

Insider Insights

"I like to see that the author has done the necessary homework to know a little about us and what kind of properties we prefer to represent," Ron Laitsch (*ron@authenticcreations.com*), of the Authentic Creations Literary Agency, Inc., in Lawrenceville, Georgia, tells us. "Something original always catches my interest. If the format of the letter has been copied from some source, it reads like so many others we see. With over 200 queries a week, we need something that makes the letter stand out. Some are clever and make us laugh, while others get to the point with information about the book. The author should always include something about his or her qualifications to write the book, including background information about any previously published materials. Something about our agency always makes us feel that the author has at least looked at our background to see if we might be a good fit for the author's work."

Our publisher, Adams Media, accepts submissions directly from authors, including first-time authors, as well as from literary agents. Adams's Web site, *www.adamsmedia.com*, lists where proposals should be sent and advises authors:

Your proposal should include the following:

- A description of the intended market for the book
- An explanation of why someone would want to buy the book
- A summary of the author's background
- A table of contents, as detailed as possible
- A sample chapter

Do not send in the whole manuscript.

We are not accepting electronic submissions at this time.

We will contact you only if we are interested in your proposal.

If you wish to have any material returned, include a self-addressed and stamped envelope. We accept no responsibility for proposals and manuscripts.

The volume of submissions does not allow us to accept phone calls or e-mail or other inquiries, or to provide comments or feedback on unsolicited manuscripts.

Learning about Publishers

Every publisher has submission policies that may differ from those at other houses. So carefully check each company's Web site and tailor your submissions to each publisher's requirements. Individualize all submissions; one size does not fit all!

While you're visiting a publisher's Web site, browse around. Familiarize yourself with the company. Examine its online catalog; learn which books and writers it published, the topics in which it specializes, and any sales figures they disclose. Check out the company's press releases and other reports about its news and developments.

Each publisher has a vision of the types of books it wants to publish and the direction in which it hopes to go. Companies' visions are usually apparent from the books they have published and some state their vision on their Web site and in the guidebooks. Publishers primarily want books that fit with what they did in the past and what they want to do in the future. Investigating each publisher will give you a feel for the house's vision and how you should shape your proposal. Consider your investigation a fact-finding mission and remember that even the most trivial information could prove invaluable in your voyage through the publishing process.

About Agents

Although agents aren't as difficult to hook up with as publishers are, they can be hard to reach and have stiff demands for authors' submissions. Study each agency's Web site before you contact it. Make a list of the agents who handle the type of book you want to pitch, and print out each agency's submission requirements. Then, follow them!

The principal way to reach an agent is via a query letter or e-mail. See Chapter 6 for a discussion of query letters and e-mails.

Some literary agents take unsolicited telephone calls, but it's usually best to call an agent only when you have a strong personal introduction.

Even then, you may not be able to get through. Agents tightly screen their calls, so don't be surprised if whoever initially answers your call, as well as all subsequent intermediaries, act as if you're asking to borrow money. Screeners are charged with protecting agents like royalty; it's a critical part of their job. So make everyone's life easier by knowing precisely what you want to say and practicing it until you can express it quickly and clearly.

Screeners have to pass your messages on to others, so being able to convey a short, clear message can be crucial. Don't let screeners throw or discourage you; some tend to be overly efficient and even officious. Many feel like it's a part of their job to impress upon you how important and busy the agent is and how fortunate you will be to speak with him or her. In most cases, screeners will instruct you to send them a query letter or e-mail, but occasionally, they will put you through.

If you reach an agent by phone, be quick, clear, and precise. Explain what your book is about in no more than fifteen to twenty seconds. Then be prepared to follow up by describing your qualifications in even less time. Remember, agents and editors are pressed for time, so be as brief as possible unless the agent makes it clear that he or she wants to talk.

To prepare for conversations with agents, make two lists, one that sets forth five or six strengths of your book, including the size of its potential market, and one that explains how your book differs from comparable books that have been published.

Don't volunteer additional information unless it becomes clear that your contact wants to talk and learn more. Concentrate on giving information about your book and you. If the agent interrupts you during your speech, don't adamantly press on. Stop speaking; listen; and if you are questioned, give a prompt, direct response. Don't move back to your pitch until you feel that the agent is satisfied with your answer.

Many agents will not accept unsolicited queries, proposals, or manuscripts via postal mail and will discard them unopened. If your e-mail query stirs their interest, they may contact you to request a hard copy of your proposal or manuscript or to talk.

Action Steps

1. *Be honest.* Does the world need another book on your topic? Check bookstores and get in the know about what books exist. If you think that your book is better and brighter, then perhaps it's meant to be.

2. *Don't let anyone talk you out of your dream.* If you believe in your idea and it does not exist, then don't postpone success. Many agents have turned down ideas and said, "It's just a magazine article," but those ideas sold.

3. *Search online.* Search everywhere. Talk to bookstore owners; see what's out there. Study your competition. Learn what other authors have done. Were their books successful?

4. *Research your book's title.* You might be surprised to find that your title already exists. Was it on your topic? The same title could be used for a book for kids and one about pets. Don't rule out a great title, but make sure that your book won't be confused with or be considered derivative to another book unless that's your intent.

5. *Create an outline.* Outline your book and see if you are still glued to the project after you set up what your chapters are about, etc. Sometimes people discover they really don't have a great deal to say, whereas others find the proof in the outline.

6. *Write a Dear Reader letter.* Try this assignment: Write a letter to your reader and state what you plan to deliver in your book. It's a promise to the reader. You'll know after writing this letter and sharing it with others if there's a burning passion in you to write this book. Then, keep your promise!

Remember:

🔺 **Before starting your book proposal, make sure that you have a strong book concept, an interesting approach, and a catchy title.** Clearly identify your market, your niche, and understand what your proposal is intended to achieve. Make sure that your book is of the best quality: that it is interesting, well written, and filled with information that will really help readers.

⚠ **Learn about agents, who serve as the gatekeepers for publishing houses.** Start by networking with friends, family, business contacts, teachers, other writers, and personnel at bookstores and libraries. Look for their names in books you like and admire. Carefully research agents and publishing houses in guidebooks and on their Web sites. Find out how they want to be contacted and what they want you to submit. Then start to think like a published author.

CHAPTER 5

The Publishing Process Explained

THIS CHAPTER WILL COVER:

▶ Initial queries
▶ Proposals
▶ Approvals
▶ Postapproval
▶ Visuals
▶ Promotion

IN ORDER TO PREPARE the best submissions, it's essential to understand the steps that are typically involved in the publishing process. When you are aware of the procedures that most publishers follow and what will be expected of you, it can increase your prospects of selling your book. Naturally, the publishing process differs from house to house, but most publishers follow a similar overall path.

Publishers may also vary in the manner in which they treat agented and unagented submissions. However, editors usually give agented submissions more and prompter attention than proposals submitted directly by writers. Editors give agented submissions priority because they have been screened by professionals and stand a better chance of being the types of projects they want.

The publishing process begins with a submission to the publishing house. Most of the time, the first submission is a query letter or e-mail, but it can also be a proposal or the author's manuscript itself.

Initial Queries

Some agents and publishing companies do not accept unsolicited submissions. So check the submission requirements on their Web site before you send anything to them.

Address your initial submissions to specific editors. Those that are not addressed to specific individuals are routed to the appropriate editors via in-house channels. They can be easily lost or misplaced.

Query letters are the preferred initial submissions, but e-mail inquiries are rapidly gaining popularity with many editors. Some editors have told us that they dislike e-mail inquiries because they interrupt their workflow and can mysteriously disappear in the blizzard of daily e-mails they receive.

Many editors shy away from unagented submissions. They tend to pawn them off on their assistants or don't read them because experience has taught them that few will be of interest.

E-mail queries tend to be responded to more promptly. However, editors tell us that a surprisingly large number are sent to editors who do not handle books on the subject of the inquiry. If an e-mail query is sent to an inappropriate editor, the recipient usually will either give the sender the name of the proper editor or forward the e-mail to that editor.

When the query letter reaches the appropriate editor, the editor will read it and usually take one of the following options:

1. Ask the writer to submit a proposal,
2. Inform the writer that he or she is not interested, or
3. Request more information from the writer. If, after receiving the requested information, the editor is still interested, he or she will usually ask the writer to submit a proposal.

Editors have standard rejection letters that they send. On occasion, however, they will give writers suggestions on how to strengthen the project.

Proposals

Proposals go through many hands. Upon receiving a proposal, editors or their editorial assistants read it. At many houses, all editors read proposals, as do the marketing and sales people. Publishers also read proposals.

If they find that the proposal has merit, they will inform their boss, who will then read and evaluate the proposal. In some firms, assistants write readers' reports, which are attached to all proposals that they forward to their bosses.

"Smart writers understand that a proposal must present the meat and potatoes of their book idea. When the proposal process begins, many first-time authors fail to produce proposals that reveal something new, innovative, and fresh. Nonfiction writers must share their revelations, unique premises, breakthroughs, and special understandings to warrant book contracts. The same goes for fiction and children's book proposals: It's all about the core idea of the book itself. So, if you're pitching a mystery novel, let them know about the fabulous surprise ending you've got.

"Having written many proposals over the years, I've found that many authors fail to develop an approach, a clear sequential program, or creative idea that will separate them from the pack. In a book proposal, the reader must be carefully guided through the book, word by word. The proposal should convince the publisher you're capable of conducting that journey.

"Editors are sifting through an enormous haystack every day, looking for that one needle. If your proposal doesn't demonstrate that you have a thorough understanding of a topic that will benefit readers, it won't capture the publisher's interest. Your proposal is your calling card for success. Show up with something unique and attention grabbing, and then you, too, can be one of the very fortunate writers who get published."

It may take weeks after a proposal is submitted for a writer to receive a response, because editors, like most other publishing employees, are usually swamped with work. Editors have the power to reject submissions upon reading them or to recommend them. Even if they like a proposal, it usually must receive additional approvals.

An editor who believes the firm should publish the proposed book becomes its champion. Some companies require proposals to be initially tested in an idea meeting.

Your goal: Whether you use an agent or submit it yourself, search for an in-house hero . . . a champion for your book! Find someone who believes in it and will push for its purchase by the house. "Books aren't bought by publishers; they're bought by editors," according to New Haven agent Don Gastwirth. So try to find your book's champion.

Behind Closed Doors

Idea meetings are usually attended by a combination of a publisher's editorial and marketing people, and the attendance may vary by who is available on any given day. Although they may be scheduled for the same day and time each week, these meetings are basically informal and unstructured, more like group discussions. They usually don't have a written schedule or agenda; everyone sits around a table and the atmosphere is collegial, relaxed, and frank.

Editors inform the group about book proposals to generate discussions in which everyone chimes in. The group asks questions, gives opinions, and volunteers information about similar or competitive books. Idea meetings are essentially exploratory. Their purpose is to challenge proposals by closely examining them and chipping away to see if the proposed project would make a good book for the house to publish. They discuss whether they think the firm should commit further time and resources to each book discussed. At idea meetings, proposals can be rejected, but they cannot be given final approval.

At these meetings, the group wants to see if the book has a strong hook and how it is positioned. The proposal must clearly answer the following questions:

- What is the book about?
- Is there an audience for the book? If so, who is that audience?
- Where will it be shelved? Books that don't have clearly identifiable places on bookstore shelves get lost. Booksellers don't know where to place them, and potential buyers don't know where to find them.
- Can the book be produced so that it provides value for readers? For example, if all the books on a subject are priced in the $30 range, can the publisher deliver this book with a higher word count or information not in competing books and sell it for $12.95?

"A book has to be clearly identifiable as something new in the marketplace," according to Gary Krebs, the publishing director at Adams Media. "New in the marketplace means that it can be on the same topic as something that already exists, but there has to be a new spin, a new direction, which sometimes can be just a format change. Or, you could spin an existing topic for a new demographic such as businesswomen when all the other books were primarily aimed at men."

All decisions are market driven; the group must believe that the book proposed can make the company money. Editors as well as marketing representatives usually won't support a proposal unless they believe that the book can be commercially viable.

If the proposal survives the idea meeting, the editor who championed it usually prepares a presentation report or packet for another committee; one that has the authority to acquire the property. The report or packet includes research on sales figures, competing books, comparable history of the publisher's other books, recent publishing trends, and whether this proposal fits in with its overall vision of what they did in the past and want to do in the future.

At many houses, the champion prepares a profit-and-loss statement (P&L) for each proposed book. If the company decides to make an offer to buy the book, the P&L statement forms the basis for the price the company will be willing to pay for the book.

Approvals

At most publishing houses, the final purchasing decision is made by the editor in chief, the chief operating officer, or an executive committee. The names of these executive committees differ for each publishing house and include editorial, acquisition, purchase, publishing committees or boards. For our purposes, let's just refer to them as publishing boards.

A publishing board usually meets at the same time each week. It consists of the publisher, editors, and marketing people. It also can include design and promotion personnel. These boards can range in size from ten to thirty people.

In some companies, the chief operating officer makes the final purchasing decision. Usually, he or she wants everyone on the committee or board to agree, but he or she will often proceed without unanimous approval. Publishing boards set the price that they will be willing to pay for the book and then the publisher sends a contract to the author's agent or directly to the author if he or she is not represented.

In publishing houses, financial thresholds exist that limit what editors or groups of editors can offer writers for books. To exceed that threshold, they usually have to get approval from the chief financial officer or someone high on the corporate ladder. If you expect top money, your proposal will get a rigorous reading from the higher-ups, who function as investment managers.

You, your agent, and the publisher then negotiate the terms of the contract and sign the deal. If you sold the book on the basis of a proposal, you must now write the manuscript. An editor is assigned to your project, and you should contact the editor to map out the direction of the book and make sure that you're both on the same page.

Postapproval

Upon completion of the manuscript and submission of it to the publisher, your editor edits the book. The editor then contacts you with his or her suggestions, to which you respond. In our experience, editors' suggestions have been greatly beneficial and have enhanced our books. At times, certain editors' opinions may be hard to swallow, but they're usually on target. Most editors are extremely professional and will improve your book.

Occasionally, an editor's suggestions will be off the wall or will move the manuscript in a direction unacceptable to the author. If this occurs and you can't work it out with the editor, summon your agent to duke it out. It's part of the service you are paying for.

When you finish making the agreed-upon revisions, your editor will accept your manuscript. At this point, a substantial portion of the advance against royalties is usually payable, frequently half.

If the book is produced in-house, the edited manuscript is sent to the production department. Frequently, production, which includes copyediting, design, and indexing, is outsourced. When these functions are subcontracted, someone in-house reviews them.

After the book is copyedited, the manuscript is sent back to you with the editor's query marks. When copyeditors' queries are transmitted via a computer file, they must be answered by using an electronic editing feature, which is available in most word-processing programs. Otherwise, copyedits are sent by hardcopy and must be attended to by hand. You must address each of the copyeditor's queries and then send the manuscript back.

Visuals

When the copyedits are agreed upon, the book design process begins. Book design primarily involves two distinct elements: the cover design and the interior design. Publishers frequently have several alternative

"Despite the conglomerate takeovers and consolidations, publishing remains a people-driven business. Machines may print, bind, and deliver books, but the key decisions on what books to publish are still made by living, breathing people. At every step in the publishing process, decisions must be made and people must make them.

"Publishing has always been a work-intensive business, and consolidation and job losses have made it more so. Although publishing industry personnel are underpaid and overworked, they have become brilliant multitaskers."

covers designed, which they test market. Among those they consult are large booksellers, mainly retail chains. Cover design is critical because readers do judge books by their covers! The book's spine is also important. The spine can be vital because most books are displayed in bookstores spine out. If the title cannot be clearly and easily read, book sales will suffer.

Since readers frequently leaf through books they are interested in, the interior book's design is also key. Books with narrow margins and small type that are jammed densely with words are intimidating and off-putting to potential readers. Volumes with wider margins, larger type, illustrations, bullets, boxes, call-outs, and white space are much more inviting. Plus, well-designed books are easier and more enjoyable for readers, which enhances both the writer's and the publisher's reputation, which can translate into dollars.

If your book involves visual content such as pictures, photographs, or illustrations, check the publisher's other books before you sign on. Try to negotiate a clause in your contract that gives you some input into the final design. Unless you're a renowned artist or designer, publishers won't give you design or visual approval. The most they will do is agree to consult with you on these matters. If you're concerned about the quality of reproduction in your book, go only with a publisher that has a consistent history of producing top-quality visual books.

Promotion

The promotional campaign for your book is usually developed by your editor and the publisher's sales and publicity departments. Although publishing houses excel at many elements of the book-production cycle, publicity is usually not their forte. Therefore, most savvy authors hire outside book publicists to work with their publisher's publicity people.

Get Involved

In today's highly competitive book-selling market, authors' involvement in the promotion of their books is essential. In fact, publishers look for authors who have platforms. Having a platform means regularly speaking before groups where they can sell their books; appearing on TV or radio; writing articles, columns, or books; teaching workshops, classes, or seminars; and having extensive lists of names.

Publishers expect their authors to dedicate themselves to working to sell their books. So your willingness and ability to promote your book can play a large role in a publisher's acquisition decision.

Company Personnel

The publishing process that we just described may seem mechanical. As you move through the publishing process, it's important not to overlook an often-undervalued part of the process: the people—publishing company personnel. Since the corporate imprint and the need to be profitable dominate most publishing companies, the unique nature of most publishing company personnel often gets overlooked.

So as you navigate the publishing waters, keep in mind that:

1. Industry personnel tend to be highly dedicated individuals who love the written word and literature. Few work for publishing

houses just for the money. Those who are entranced by publishing's glamour or cachet generally don't last long, but those who love language and books often do. Somehow, some way, they find ways to remain. Dealing with kindred spirits who are committed to quality books and writing is a bonanza for writers because it can improve their work and enhance the entire publishing experience as well as their lives. Few experiences are as satisfying as working with people who share your vision and values! It's exhilarating.

2. Publishing company employees change jobs frequently. The editor who championed your book and fought for it in the editorial board may move on to another publisher or end up selling kitchen fixtures. Suddenly, you may feel alone, abandoned, and discouraged. Hang in there because chances are that a good or even better replacement will emerge. When these situations occur, the value of a good agent takes on heightened importance. Your agent can intercede with the publisher on your behalf to get you a top replacement. Your agent can also serve as your advisor and confidant and provide much of the support that your editor lent.

Action Steps

1. *Become a proposal-writing authority.* Consider your proposal the business plan for your book. You wouldn't open a business without a plan. The same goes for a book.

2. *Begin!* Write a page or two a day. No excuses. If you can't make time to write at least a page or so a day, what makes you think you will be able to write a book?

3. *Be critical.* Avoid falling blindly in love with your own ideas. Run them by people you trust. Don't go too far on your book without talking to people in the know.

4. *In writing your proposal, think like your readers.* Is your book interesting? A great read? Life changing? Think like an editor. Is your

book clear and well written? Who will buy it? When you review what you write, ask lots of questions.

5. *Check out examples of proposals.* Is your proposal convincing? Is it your best shot? Does it include third-party endorsements? What can you add to it to make it a heavyweight proposal? Lightweights don't sell.

Remember:

⚠ **Check whether agents or publishers accept unsolicited submissions.** Address your initial submissions to specific individuals, not generally, or they may not be delivered. Most agents and editors want the first contact from writers to be by query letters, and most of them now welcome e-mail inquiries.

⚠ **Individual editors initially process proposals. If they feel a proposal has promise, they take it to committees where it will be examined in great detail.** Editors, their assistants, sales and marketing people, and the top brass generally review proposals. At most houses, the final acquisition decision is made by the editor in chief, the chief operating officer, or an executive committee, and it is invariably financially based.

chapter 6

"There are three rules for writing the novel. Unfortunately, no one knows what they are."

W. Somerset Maugham

Query Letters

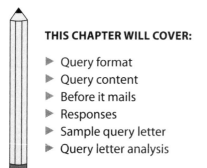

THIS CHAPTER WILL COVER:

▶ Query format
▶ Query content
▶ Before it mails
▶ Responses
▶ Sample query letter
▶ Query letter analysis

IN PUBLISHING, the accepted protocol to start the book-acquisition process is sending a query asking agents or editors if they would be interested in your project. Query letters or e-mails should be submitted to literary agents if you're looking for an agent to represent you, or to editors if you want to go directly to a publisher. Queries should be submitted for all books: fiction, nonfiction, children's books, art books, cookbooks, whatever.

When you compile a list of agents' and editors' names, send them query letters or e-mails. Even those who accept unsolicited telephone inquiries prefer a written query because it gives them a sense of how well you write. If recipients are interested in a project, they will initiate further contact. How you initially query an agent or editor is critical. Your query is your chance to make a strong first impression and generate interest in you and your project. So, it's vital to do it well. If you don't, you may not get another shot.

Publishers and agents have different specialties and submission requirements, which can frequently change. Before you send a query letter, check your target's Web site so you don't send your how-to book to an agent who handles fiction, or an editor who now works for a different publishing house. Most publishers and agents list their submission requirements on their Web site, so frame your queries as they suggest.

As the name indicates, the main purpose of a query letter is to inquire if an agent or editor would be interested in learning more about your book. Your query has to arouse the agent's or editor's interest and make him or her want to see more. To capture the agent's or editor's attention, your inquiry has to clearly demonstrate that you have a great idea for a book that will sell and that you're professional and disciplined and write well. Query letters show agents and editors that you:

- Have a good idea for a salable book that is compatible with their areas of interest or list
- Can express yourself clearly in writing
- Have the ability and qualifications to complete your book
- Are professional

The agent or the editor who receives your submission will make a quick assessment of your professionalism on the basis of that submission.

Rick Says

"Never underestimate the importance of demonstrating your professionalism. Agents and publishers want to work with writers who have their act together, who are focused, result oriented, and willing to do what it takes to write and support a successful book. Working with professionals makes their lives easier; it cuts down on the possibilities that writers will not follow directions, that their submissions will be late, will be delivered in poor shape, and will require more in-house work. Agents and publishers prefer to deal with writers whom they can rely on to deliver a quality book."

If your submission comes in a colorful package or is written on colorful stationery; has flowery stamps; contains cross-outs, typos, and misspellings; or is generally sloppy in appearance, recipients will label you unprofessional. If they don't reject your submission, they will probably delay reading it or will assign it to an underling.

To make a strong initial impression, submit a professional-looking query letter!

Do It Like the Pros Do!

For query letters use:

- A business-type letterhead that gives your name and contact information.
- Basic white or off-white 8½ x 11-inch paper.
- A standard typeface that can be read easily. Avoid script or other typefaces that are difficult to read.
- 10- or 12-point type.
- Black ink.
- Margins of 1½ inches at the top and bottom and at least 1 inch on the sides.
- Include a self-addressed, stamped envelope with the proper amount of postage.

All enclosures should be typed on good quality paper stock and in black ink. Don't get fancy or, worse yet, cute. Avoid bold colors, gimmicky borders, or other features that could distract from your message.

Strive for brevity and clarity. Make your letters short, well written, and to the point. Your main objective should be to get your foot in the door, to make an agent or publisher curious and ask for more about your book. The best way to do so is to clearly and professionally communicate the specialness of your book idea in plain, straightforward, easily understood English.

Make sure your letter isn't headed for immediate rejection: "An immediate turnoff is when I receive an inquiry that shows that the writer hasn't done enough research," agent Edward Knappman, of New England Publishing Associates, explains. "If I get an inquiry regarding a novel, it's obvious that they haven't done enough research to learn that we don't handle fiction. If they haven't researched our agency, the first thing I ask is, 'How can they do enough research for the book?'"

Another instant turnoff occurs when the agent's name or the firm's name is misspelled. Remarkably, agents inform us, such misspellings are all too common.

Query Format

Before you send a query letter, always check the agent's or publisher's Web site for instructions or samples regarding what you should send. Most will state exactly what they want, but some could be vague. If the requirements are not clear, follow these formats:

For *nonfiction* books, try to keep query letters to a single page, and don't exceed two pages. Always include all your contact information and a self-addressed, stamped envelope.

Query letters for *fictional* works also should not exceed a single page. They should include an outline, a synopsis or a summary of your book, and sample chapters or the completed manuscript. Agents and editors differ on how long the synopsis should run: Some want only a page or two whereas others will accept as many as five or six pages. Err on the side of brevity. Since the agents and editors will be judging the quality of your writing, show in your synopsis that you can clearly and concisely describe your book in two or three pages. Delete all extraneous details and hone your synopsis until it's tight.

As for samples of your fiction, submit as much as you can to demonstrate the quality of your work. Some agents and editors request the submission of only two or three sample chapters, but most want the entire manuscript. Show your belief in your work by submitting as much as you have completed. As with nonfiction, always enclose a self-addressed, stamped envelope with sufficient postage or you probably won't get your submission back.

For all e-mail queries, fiction and nonfiction:

- Write no more than a single screen.
- Don't send e-mail attachments unless they are specifically requested, because they probably won't be opened otherwise, due to concerns about computer security.
- Use the same high standards for e-mail queries that you use for print submissions because the recipients will judge them with equal severity.

In some agencies, e-mail queries face more challenges than postal submissions do because they're reviewed by a number of screeners and must be outstanding to reach a decision maker. Conversely, postal mail queries that are addressed to the decision maker usually travel a shorter, less-arduous route before they get through.

Query letters stand a good chance of being read simply because they're short. If they run long, they run the risk of being skimmed or even disregarded. So craft your query letters carefully and make them brief. If parties are interested, they will request more information.

Feel free to send query letters to more than one agent or publisher at a time; agents simultaneously send proposals to multiple publishers. If an agent shows interest and requests a proposal or manuscript, he or she may also ask for the exclusive right to read or sell your book. If you agree to a reading exclusive, make it for a short term not longer than a month or six weeks. An exclusive agreement for an agent to sell your work should be in writing and should be cancelable by either party on thirty days' written notice.

"Write a professional, nongimmicky letter about how and why this project will sell and to whom it is targeted. We're in the business to make money, so if you can point out how your project will make my company money, you will get my attention," Jennifer Enderlin points out.

Addressing Your Letter

When you forward query letters to publishers or agents, direct them to specific individuals, not to companies, "Editors," "Gentlemen," "Dear Sirs or Madams," and so on. Publishing houses and literary agencies are often large, and imprecisely addressed mailings can get lost. Busy, overworked employees may also seize upon any excuse not to open another envelope.

Address every submission to a specific recipient or it probably won't be opened or receive sufficient attention. Also, triple-check the spelling of *all* names, individuals, and firms, because misspelling an agent's or editor's name could fast-track your submission to oblivion.

Query Content

A nonfiction query letter must include:

1. **A tight lead sentence describing your book.** The lead sentence should be a grabber that hooks the reader and makes him or her want to read further. So sculpt your lead artfully. Give the title, length, and what the book is about. Questions/answers, statistics, and anecdotes can also make effective opening sentences. Explain why you selected this agent or publisher to query. It could be that the agent or publisher was recommended to you by one of their authors, or that you loved a book he or she handled, which you feel is similar to your title. Agents and editors may respond more favorably to writers who have done their homework and know something about them and their work.

   Keep your lead to two or two and a half lines. If you need to round off your lead or to add other crucial information that didn't fit in your lead, add another short sentence, no more than a line or two. If you have celebrity status, work it into the lead or second sentence.

2. **A paragraph or two supporting and amplifying the lead.**
    a. Provide more details on:
        i. The subject of the book,
        ii. Why your book is special or how it differs from other books,
        iii. The market for the book,
        iv. How the book is organized or formatted, and
        v. Why it will interest editors.
    b. Point out problems that your book will solve and concrete ways that it will help readers.
    c. Include facts or statistics that show the size of your book's potential market.
    d. State whether the manuscript has been written or when you expect to complete it.

3. **Your biography.** Don't just use your standard resume or only stress your educational and business background, but show why you're so uniquely qualified to write this book. Include your past writing credits, awards in your field, and your platform. Sell them, don't just tell them!

4. **A summary statement.** Thank the recipient for his or her time and offer to send additional materials such as a proposal, sample chapters, or the manuscript.

Remember that in a query letter, brevity and clarity are essential.

"If you can't spit it out clearly, there's a problem," New York agent Liv Bloomer, of the Bloomer Literary Agency, says. "Often, people are too close to their own material to be able to give a clear description of the big picture. Someone in a recent query said, 'It's really very hard to describe my book.' Then it's a clear sign that the author has problems, because it will be hard to pass the message along."

"The person needs to have the ability to describe the project in terms of the big picture or in a clear overview instead of giving every detail that's in the book," Bloomer continues. "In every step of the life

Robyn Says

"Write a sound bite for your book, which many call an 'elevator speech' because it can be delivered in the time it takes to go from the first to the second floor. Your sound bite should give a brief description that you can reel off in ten to fifteen seconds. You can use it when you query agents and editors, write book proposals, and tell others about your book.

"When you write your sound bite, remember the observation of theater impresario David Belasco: 'If you can't write your idea on the back of my calling card, you don't have a clear idea.'"

of a book, there are a couple of dozen people who have to sell it to somebody. The message gets watered down as it passes from sales hand to sales hand: the person selling to the bookstores, the person selling to foreign publishers, whoever it may be. If the message cannot be delivered clearly and briefly, someone is going to get it wrong. And by the end, it doesn't resemble your book anymore."

Don't stuff your query letter mailings with other materials such as your table of contents, sample chapters, or loads of biographical information. If you send bulky packages, they may not be opened. Instead, offer to send a proposal containing those items and enclose a self-addressed, stamped envelope. A query letter for fiction must:

1. **Start with a great lead sentence that gives a clear overview of what the story is about.** Try to write the lead sentence in no more than two lines. Craft the lead to stir up interest, create excitement, and make the recipient eager to read the sample chapters or manuscript enclosed. Your lead sentence should contain the most important information about your book. Then, if necessary, follow it up with a sentence or two, still in the opening paragraph, that gives other essential information.
2. **In two or three paragraphs, amplify and expand on the descriptions in the first paragraph.** Provide a general overview

and don't go into exhaustive plot detail. If the book contains a riveting or surprising ending, describe it briefly. Avoid overkill. Fiction writers are frequently so immersed in their books that they describe them in excessive depth. Ask friends, editors, or other writers to review your queries before you mail them, to make sure that you didn't go overboard in describing your book.

3. **Toward the end of the query, briefly describe your book's structure, format, or any special features.** Identify the market for your book and provide information about yourself, including your writing credits, your background, and a summary of your platform. Briefly mention your promotional ideas or plans.

Remember that in a query letter, brevity and clarity are essential. Keep it to one written page or computer screen.

"Going into a lot of plot detail is a huge mistake," according to agent Liv Bloomer. "With fiction, all I really want to know is who, what, when, where. Tell me where it's set, tell me when it's set and give me the big overview. Don't tell me that she did this, then she did this, and then she bought a dress." Instead, you should just lay out the basic story, give the big picture.

An Instant Turnoff!

"It's really important to let agents know if you've simultaneously submitted your work to multiple agents or if he or she is the only agent looking at it," Agent Bonnie Solow reports. "It also helps for me to know the history of the project to date—has it been shopped to editors or agents. If so, to whom and what happened. Some authors don't reveal that the book has already gone to twenty publishers. I've heard of cases where agents have spent time reading, editing, or developing projects and then unknowingly submitted them to editors who had already rejected them.

"I also want to know about any changes or revisions they've made since the book was rejected," Solow continues. "If not in the query or cover letter, in our first direct conversation."

Keep a copy of all queries and enclosures. Never send one-of-a-kind artwork or enclosures that cannot be duplicated or replaced. Include a self-addressed envelope with the proper postage for all enclosures that you would like returned. Always provide all of your contact information: your name, address, e-mail address, and telephone and fax numbers.

Before It Mails

Carefully proofread everything you send. Typos, misspellings, and grammatical mistakes are the kiss of death. So are sloppy-looking submissions that have spots, smudges, stains, creases, or cross-outs. Focus on showing that you're an accomplished, professional writer that the publisher or agent can trust. Check each letter by:

- Letting it sit overnight after you complete it and then printing it out the following day when you can read it with refreshed eyes. If you make changes the next day, hold it to reread for one additional day.
- Having a reliable copyeditor read it.
- Checking that the pages are numbered correctly. Don't rely on a printer; check all page numbers yourself. Pages can get mixed up when you make copies. Remember, every detail counts.
- Sending every e-mail query letter to yourself, printing it out the next day and then reading it before you send it to agents or editors. Make your final read from a hard copy printout, not the computer screen. When you read from the screen, problems can easily be missed.

Don't send a query until you have a book proposal already prepared. If an editor or agent requests that you submit a proposal, be in a position to quickly capitalize on his or her interest, while your query is still fresh in his or her mind. Since editors and agents receive so many inquiries, distinguish yourself and show your professionalism by getting a killer proposal back to them by return mail (or electronically if they so request).

Responses

When they get query letters, most agents and editors don't have time to comment on your project and give you constructive feedback, so don't expect it. However, some may comment on your query and even give you suggestions. If they like something about you or your project, they may also tell you to contact them again.

Value whatever feedback you get. Savvy agents and editors know the market and the slants or directions they suggest can improve your book and the chances of its selling. In addition, it's usually easier to accept feedback at the query-letter stage than it is after you have written an extensive proposal, chapters, or even an entire manuscript.

If agents or publishers are interested in your query, they will probably respond to you within a few weeks. For sixty days, don't call, write or send e-mail asking whether they received your letter. After sixty days, write a brief inquiry note or e-mail. Also, don't send stuff that you forgot to include or think might influence their decision. Just wait, and if you get no response within a month, move on.

Sample Query Letter

Query letters should vary according to the nature and unique qualities of each book idea presented. Use the sample that we have provided on the next page as a guide to get the general idea of how a query letter should be structured and what it should contain. Then adapt it to your own particular circumstances.

Before each item in the sample query letter below, numbers have been inserted that correspond with numbers in the following section,

"Query Letter Analysis." We will discuss the points that correspond to those numbers in "Query Letter Analysis." Please note that the letter below and the information in it are fictional.

---

(1) November 15, 2005

(2) Re: Query about *How to Fire Employees Without Getting Sued*

(3) Dear _____:

(4) Fired employees are now suing their ex-employers in record numbers and juries are awarding them unprecedented damage amounts. Insurance premiums have skyrocketed and experts warn that the flood hasn't crested. As an attorney and writer who specializes in employment law, I wrote *How to Fire Employees Without Getting Sued* to help the millions of small business operators who could suffer from this trend. I hope you will be interested in my book, which will run about 210 pages.

(5) Employment-related lawsuits now account for 25 percent of the cases brought in federal courts. Employers lose roughly two out of three employment practice suits that go to trial, and that's not counting those that are settled out of court, which can cost employers millions. In California, the average wrongful termination jury award is reported to be $1.3 million, and employers still have to foot the bill for their legal expenses. Trial costs for employment practice suits are said to average $450,000. Jurors tend to sympathize with fired workers and frequently punish employers by handing out huge awards that can bankrupt small businesses. Even if employers win or reach quick settlements, defending former employees' claims is expensive, time-consuming, and disruptive to their businesses and personal lives.

---

(6) The primary market for *How to Fire Employees* is small businesses that do not have in-house human relations departments. This represents a market of 5 million in the United States alone. Since the book contains so many universal business principles, it will also have a wide appeal with larger companies. It will also be of great help to small partnerships and single proprietors who are interested in hiring others. Approximately one half of the book has been completed, and it will take three months to complete the balance of the book.

(7) I have been a practicing attorney for seventeen years, during which I have specialized in employment law. My practice is evenly divided between representing employers and employees, so I know both sides. I write a monthly e-mail newsletter called *The Law at Work* and a monthly column for the *Seaboard Law Journal* entitled "At the Workplace." I have also been the keynote speaker at the 2005 Annual Convention of the Employers League. I am a graduate of Rutgers University School of Law and am in private practice in Washington, D.C.

(8) Thank you for considering *How to Fire Employees Without Getting Sued*, and I look forward to hearing from you. I will be happy to send you a book proposal or other information that you may request. A self-addressed stamped envelope is included for your convenience.

Sincerely,
(9) A. Lawrence Lawson
27 Clode Terrace
Calonia, CA
05555
(10) Phone: 555-555-5555
Fax: 555-555-5556
(11) E-mail: alawson@email.com

Query Letter Analysis

(1) The date is helpful for filing and record keeping. It also gives you reference points with regard to response time and other factors that could be helpful down the road.

(2) In the reference line, state what the letter is about so the recipients can forward it to the right personnel and easily file and access it.

(3) As we previously stated, query letters should be sent to specific individuals, not to companies, unnamed "Editors," "Gentlemen," "Dear Sirs or Madams," or "Publisher." Unspecific mailings are easily misplaced or may not be opened.

(4) The lead paragraph is critical. In a minimum of words, clearly explain the purpose of your letter. Start with gripping information, facts, or a quote. Or begin by stating, "I would like to submit a proposal" and then vividly describe your book. Include the title of your book and put it in italics. In your lead, hook the reader by describing the spirit or essence of your book. State the most important information that an agent or publisher should know about the book in the lead. Either give your page count or some indication of the size of your book. Keep the lead paragraph to two or three sentences because agents and publishers will want to see if you write crisply and succinctly.

(5) Use the second paragraph to round out your initial description of the book. Provide the next most important information in order to more graphically paint the picture that you want to convey.

(6) In paragraph three, stress the market for the book. Since a query letter is primarily a marketing document that is intended to sell your book, describe the size of the market. When possible, give statistics that justify the size of your potential market. Let agents and publishers see dollar signs, because books become more attractive when they see the opportunity to make money.

In the third paragraph, also describe the status of your book and how long you think it will take to complete. You can also explain how your book is organized and/or designed and any other special features. If the book has been completed, say so. If it has been professionally edited, add that too. Agents tell us that professionally edited manuscripts receive a much better reception.

(7) In paragraph four, state your qualifications and describe your platform. Shape your personal information to show why you are so uniquely qualified to write this book.

(8) Thank the agent or publisher for his or her interest and offer to send a book proposal or additional information. Enclose a self-addressed, stamped envelope.

(9) (10) (11) Give all your contact information, your entire postal address, telephone and fax numbers, and e-mail address. Let the recipient decide how to contact you.

Carefully reread and edit your query letter. Double-check all of your spelling and triple-check all numbers and Web addresses, including your own. Follow the advice that we previously gave by letting your query letter sit overnight.

Before you submit your book, print it out, and check it carefully. Then, send it off.

Action Steps

1. Write a clear opening sentence describing what your book is about. If you can't describe it in one easy sentence, think about it, wait and try again. Keep working at it; even the most difficult topic can be described.

2. Sell them, don't just tell them about your book. What are your top selling points? Be sure to list them. Consider what will motivate book sales. Authors, listen up! You are officially salespeople.

3. Share your proposal with a trusted bookstore owner and see what he or she thinks. Or perhaps ask a writing instructor or fellow writer for feedback.

4. Double-check and triple-check every word, fact, figure, and detail. Before you send it, let it sit for a day and then give it a final read with refreshed eyes.
5. Make sure to make copies of everything you send. Check all page numbers and make sure that they are in the proper order. You can never be too careful.

Remember:

⚠ **The book-acquisition process starts when you send query letters or e-mails asking agents or editors if they are interested in your project.** A nonfiction query should begin with a tight lead sentence describing the book, a paragraph or two supporting and amplifying the lead, and your biography. In the bio, show why you're so uniquely qualified to write this book.

⚠ **Make your query clear, brief, and to the point.** Carefully proofread it and make sure that it's letter perfect. Keep copies of all queries that you send and maintain a log recording when you sent them. Don't send queries until you have written a first-rate proposal and have it ready to go. That way, if agents or editors request a proposal, you can send it right off while it's still fresh in their minds.

"Author: A fool, who, not content with having bored those who have lived with him, insists on tormenting the generations to come."

Montesquieu

Proposal Basics

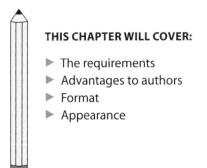

THIS CHAPTER WILL COVER:

▶ The requirements
▶ Advantages to authors
▶ Format
▶ Appearance

A PROPOSAL IS YOUR BUSINESS PLAN for selling your book. While it might be a painstaking process, it can be the key to your success.

Many authors feel that writing a book proposal is the worst and most difficult part of writing a book. Writing a proposal can be a pain because the format must adhere to a blueprint that differs from approaches most authors normally take. It often stifles an authors' freedom, and some, who write brilliantly about the most complex topics, often become completely blocked when they try to draft book proposals.

Many of us are handcuffed by book proposals because they force us to take a linear approach, which is not the way many authors work. Book ideas often spring from mysterious sources and come to us at the strangest times. When they emerge, they're frequently little more than undeveloped snippets, little germs that take forever to gel or make complete sense. Frequently, these ideas are so unformed that they can't be clearly communicated to others and all our attempts make no sense. However, they have a compelling force that won't go away and they make us smile, or give us hope, buoy our spirits, and propel us forward.

Authors are often more interested in going through the process of giving their concepts form than they are in defining them. In fact, they frequently can't or don't want to define them. So, when they're pressed to explain their thoughts in concrete terms, as they must do in book proposals, they simply can't.

From Dread to Read!

Proposals also call to mind those dreaded outlines that we tried to avoid during our school days. Although we understood the value of outlines, we hated having to formally commit ourselves to ideas that we hadn't fully thought through. Most of us preferred to wing it; we wanted to just start writing what we knew and see where it took us. Writing outlines frequently deprived us of the pleasure of exploring and working through options and potential solutions. We preferred to use our ingenuity and instincts instead of formulas.

Well, if you think that writing prescribed outlines in school was a drag, it's doubly so as an adult, and it's especially distasteful if you're an author. Since authors write so much, many tend to think that they can simply throw together a bunch of sketchy information, come up with a catchy title, and the brilliance of their prose plus the genius of their ideas will tie it all together and seal the deal.

"You have to fashion your writing to how the industry accepts it," agent and book packager John Monteleone advises. "You have to understand that a proposal is important and you have to write the hell out of it because that's what will sell your project. Unless you're a huge celebrity, publishers won't buy your book just because you present yourself. They need more to make a judgment. Understand that proposals are passed around. Although you may submit it to someone who knows lots about the subject, it will be passed on to others who don't know as much, if anything, and they have a say in whether they think the book will work for the house."

Proposals must be formulaic for good reasons. Although they can contain creative writing, they are not primarily exercises in creative writing. Their main purpose is to serve as structured documents that quickly and clearly give agents and acquisitions editors precise information. If your proposal doesn't promptly tell them what they want to know, they won't read any further and your proposal will probably be rejected. When they read proposals, agents and editors need to see that you've touched all the bases and covered all the major points that they know are essential for a successful book.

The Requirements

Book proposals have set requirements for a number of sound reasons, not simply because of agents' and publishers' arbitrary whims. Agents and book publishers are inundated with requests from aspiring writers, and they usually can only afford to pursue those that they think will sell. According to estimates, agents accept only 2 percent of the submissions they receive, or one in fifty, so they must be able to read them quickly and immediately spot the answers to their qualifying questions. From a book proposal, agents and publishers must get a quick, strong indication that:

- You have a viable book idea.
- Your book's subject matter fits their list.
- You are qualified to write the book.
- You write clearly.
- You are well organized.
- You are committed to your book project.
- You have thoroughly thought through the book project.
- You will vigorously promote your book.

Unless you're a superstar, a noted celebrity, or an established author who is a proven commodity, book proposals are the litmus tests for agents and publishers. They are the rite of passage that authors must pass in order to enter the hallowed literary halls. Book proposals are the ticket for your admission into the authors' guild.

Author Tactic

The two most important keys to writing a successful book proposal are having a positive attitude and being disciplined.

1. **Attitude.** If you want your book to reach the market, understand that the proposal is a necessary evil that you must complete. Adopt a positive attitude because your negativity could seep into or otherwise affect your writing and scare agents and publishers away. Instead of resenting the fact that you have to write a formulaic proposal and fighting it, think of your proposal as an opportunity to demonstrate your talent and expertise. See it as the chance to strut your stuff, to wow agents and publishers and knock them off their feet, and to make them compete to publish your work. Use your passion for your book and its concepts to sell them. Let your proposal showcase your talent and help you shine.

2. **Discipline.** Proposals are tests that you must pass in order to convince a publisher to buy your book. Understand the purpose of the proposal and focus on demonstrating to agents and publishers that you have the ability and fortitude to write a successful book in the context they want. Agents and publishers are wary of high-maintenance writers who don't follow the rules and cause them additional work. They know that dealing with such writers is frequently not cost-effective, can be time consuming, and certainly isn't fun. So have the discipline to give them what they want and shape your ideas and approaches to fit seamlessly with their demands.

Advantages to Authors

Although proposals can be hard to write, they provide invaluable benefits to writers. Think of them as business plans, which are documents that justify every step of a prospective commercial venture and are required to get financing for business deals.

When you want to finance a new business, you can't just say, "I have this great idea" and expect the investors to fight for a place in line. You must first prepare a convincing plan that explains, step-by-step, your idea, the need for your product or service, how it would work, and how it will make money. A business plan must hold up under the fierce scrutiny of financial experts who will question and measure every expense.

Book proposals operate similarly and serve as both planning documents and selling documents. In regard to planning, a book proposal gives you the opportunity to lay out your strategy for writing and promoting a salable book and to run it by your agent and others, who are expert at evaluating such plans. It forces you to anticipate each stage in the entire book-writing process and to decide exactly how you plan to proceed. It clarifies your approach and the resources you will need and can expose weaknesses that you should address.

Robyn Says

"Fortunately, most agents and editors are open-minded; the vast majority love and seek new ideas, expressions, and talent. They also are devoted to writing and books. However, as we have previously emphasized, publishing is a business and many voices will take part in the decision regarding whether to publish your book. Many of those voices will be from the business and marketing world and they will be primarily concerned with sales, numbers, and profits.

"Help editors to serve as your advocates and champions. Give them disciplined proposals that they can use as ammunition to convince their more business-minded colleagues about the benefits of publishing your book."

And in regard to selling, proposals enable you to present representative samples of your work that will sell your book idea to an agent or publisher. It's the marketing case that contains examples of your wares and should be stocked to convince your targets to buy. When a publisher decides to buy your book, it is basically agreeing to finance your book's publication by paying the costs of its printing and distribution.

Format

Although the formats of proposals can differ, a number of basic elements should be included in every proposal. Like most of us, agents and publishers are creatures of habit, and when they receive book proposals, they will be looking for specific information. Since a major purpose of your proposal is to sell them on your book, don't force them to hunt for the answers they need. Instead, give them what they want in a format they like and can easily follow.

In a proposal, we like to include the basic sections that are listed below. After the overview, their order can be varied to give greater prominence to a particular strength. For example, the fact that an author is a huge celebrity should be stressed in the overview and the about-the-author section should be placed directly after the overview.

The basic proposal sections we recommend for nonfiction are:

- Cover letter
- Title page
- Overview
  - Spin-offs
- Markets for the book
  - Translations
  - Products
- About the author
- Promotion plan
- Table of contents

- Chapter summaries or outline
- Introduction
- Sample chapter(s)
- Additional submissions
  - Endorsements
  - Reviews or short excerpts of your prior writing
  - Relevant articles, clippings, and press materials
- Postage-paid, self-addressed envelope. Large enough and with enough postage. Many agents won't return material if the envelope is not large enough and it doesn't contain sufficient postage.

In the following chapters, we will discuss each of these sections and provide a sample that we will analyze.

Fiction

As we've stated, most fiction written by unpublished authors doesn't reach the proposal stage. Agents and editors make acquisition decisions on the basis of queries and writing samples or manuscripts that accompany them. However, published authors may have to submit proposals to sell their subsequent books because approval by the publisher's editorial board is generally required.

So before you submit a proposal for your novel or short story book, check the publisher's Web site to learn exactly what it wants, because the requirements for various houses can differ. In addition, some publishers post helpful samples that you can follow.

If the publisher's Web site does not state precisely what you should submit, send:

- Cover letter
- Title page
- A synopsis, summary, or description of the book

- The first three chapters or the entire manuscript
- A stamped, self-addressed envelope

The cover letter should not exceed one page. It must describe the book proposed in a sentence or two and list the items that are included in the submission package. Clarity and brevity are critical in a cover letter because it is often attached to the proposal and accompanies it through the entire acquisition process.

The outline does not need to go into great detail, but it should show that the book flows logically and has a beginning, middle, and end. When the entire manuscript is submitted, an outline is optional. However, it becomes more important when just a portion of the work is submitted, because agents and editors need to see it to fill in the gaps. They need proof that the author has thought the book through, covered all the bases and organized it coherently.

Since some editors feel they can't get the true sense of a work of fiction unless they read the entire manuscript, submit as much of the book as you can, preferably the completed manuscript. That's what Robyn and Mark Johnston did for their children's book, *Secret Agent*, and here's how Susan Burke, their editor at Simon & Schuster, reacted: "As soon I saw the proposal for *Secret Agent*, I knew that it was going to

Rick Says

"Expect editors to be skeptical. They've seen and heard it all: every promise; every approach; and wild, unrealistic representation. When they receive a proposal, it can be hard for them to tell fact from fiction, so they may tend to err on the side of caution. Look at it from their perspective: if they push for a proposal, their heads can be on the line if the books fail or, worse yet, if the authors fail to deliver.

"So help acquisitions editors by giving them strong, well-reasoned, and thought-out proposals that look good and read even better. Give them something they can be excited about and willing to fight for."

be a very special project. The story was fresh, touching, funny, and told in a truly unique voice. The plot was fast paced and I knew it would appeal to both boys and girls. Generally, we ask authors to submit the first three chapters of a novel with their proposal, but in this case, the agent sent the entire manuscript of *Secret Agent*. A good rule of thumb for any aspiring writer is to send the first three chapters of a novel, along with a short summary of the entire project, along with your proposal."

Appearance

Your proposal represents you; it's your ambassador. Its appearance can cause editors to form an immediate opinion about you, your proposed manuscript, and your ability to deliver what you promise—and you know how important first impressions can be!

A clean, well-organized, and easy-to-read proposal can convince editors to place your proposal atop the heap. A sloppy submission can discourage them and indicate that you're unprofessional.

Action Steps

1. List five key items that agents and editors must see in your proposal.
2. Determine how you could improve your attitude and determination with regard to your proposal.
3. What specific material can you include in your proposal to make it a better planning document?
4. What specific information should you provide in your proposal to make it an effective selling aid?
5. Review the basic proposal sections in your mind. What additional items could strengthen your proposal?

Remember:

⚠ **A proposal should be structured to quickly and clearly give agents and acquisitions editors precise information.** If it doesn't, they may not read any further. Agents and editors need to see that the author has touched all the bases and covered all of the major points that are essential for a successful book.

⚠ **A winning book proposal must show that you have a viable book idea and that the book's subject matter will fit into the publisher's list.** It also must demonstrate that you are qualified to write the book, can write clearly, are well organized, are committed to the book project, have thoroughly thought through the project, and will vigorously promote the book.

"What is written without effort is in general read without pleasure."
Samuel Johnson

Cover Letter, Format, and Title Page

THIS CHAPTER WILL COVER:

▶ Cover letters
▶ Proposal format
▶ Title page
▶ Table of contents
▶ Proposal sections

INCLUDE A BRIEF COVER LETTER with your proposal. Check agents' or publishers' Web sites to see if they post any requirements for cover letters. Then write your letters in the manner they suggest.

The primary purpose of a cover letter is to tell the reader what you sent. A cover letter is not a second query. So, except for the title, which you should always give, don't repeat or amplify information you previously provided in your query unless you have something earth-shattering to add. Always include your contact information (your name, address, phone and fax numbers, and e-mail address).

If you have a special relationship with the agent or editor, allude to it. You might say, "Bill sends his best," or "It was wonderful speaking with you at the conference in Maui. Thanks for the great tips!" These little comments will place you in context and help separate your sub-mission from the pack, but don't go overboard! In most cases, keep your cover letters simple, direct, and short. Although we prefer brief cover letters, some firms want more. In addition to the author's contact information, they suggest including a single-paragraph summation of the book and its word count. They also think you should state whether the book has been written and if not, the projected completion date.

If you have a great platform, credentials, or media contacts, you might mention them and the promotion possibilities. For example, if you are a doctor who appeared on *Oprah,* slip it in. Show that you're promotable even if your appearance was five years ago.

Kim Weiss, the director of communications at HCI Books, thinks writers should write a killer cover letter for the proposal. "I want to be wooed early and have a reason to read more. But you have to back it up; you can't have sizzle without substance," she warns.

- Address your cover letter—as well as the entire proposal package—to the specific individual who requested it, and be succinct and courteous.
- Point out exactly what you're sending—the proposal—and clearly identify all attachments enclosed.
- Mention the title of your book.
- Thank the recipient.

Don't go into lengthy discussions in the cover letter. Let the proposal speak for itself. Think of the cover letter as being the wrapping paper covering a gift. In most cases write nothing more than:

Dear _____:

Attached is the proposal for my book *Once Upon a Time: How the Decline of Storytelling Is Damaging Society* that you requested. Thank you for giving me the opportunity to submit it to you for your consideration.

Sincerely,
Your Name

When you send important or multiple attachments with your proposal, list precisely what you've enclosed and consider bulleting each item. For example,

I am also enclosing photographs of:

- Small children farming on the banks of the Mekong River
- Sunset over Luong Prabang, Laos
- A rack of rice cakes drying in the sun

Proposal Format

Prepare your proposal in a manner that makes it simple for the agent or editor to follow. As with queries and cover letters, submit proposals on standard 8½ x 11-inch good-quality white paper, not erasable bond.

Use a standard, easy-to-read typeface, at least 12-point type, and don't get fancy or use script. Double-space, with 1½-inch margins at the top and bottom and 1-inch margins on the sides.

Print in crisp black ink, not colored ink. Since your proposal will be repeatedly photocopied, you want to minimize the generational fade. Faint copies can infuriate editors, and it makes no sense to antagonize those who have the life of your book in their hands.

Write all the words in chapter and section titles in upper- and lowercase. Number the pages continuously throughout the manuscript, not chapter by chapter.

Make your proposal easier and more reader-friendly by:

- Being consistent in your style and avoiding formats that make the type so dense that it's hard to read. Tightly packed paragraphs are off-putting and intimidating, so many won't put themselves through the unpleasantness of reading them.
- Bulleting key material whenever possible, so it jumps off the page and attracts the reader's eye. Give careful thought to the

material you highlight and don't overuse bullets or it will reduce their value.

- Breaking up long sections by inserting centered or side headings when appropriate or every three-quarters of a page or so. Headings give readers places to pause and digest what they just read.
- Writing in the third person. If you're a major celebrity or the book is about you, your experiences, observations, or theories, write in the first person. Otherwise, write in the third person.

Avoid spiral and other bindings that are hard to remove. "When a proposal comes in, it gets torn apart, photocopied, and passed from person to person. Spiral binding is a pain to remove. Although it may look good, it ends up being more of a hindrance than a help," Danielle Chiotti, acquisitions editor at Adams Media, disclosed. By all means, make your presentation look great, but don't saddle busy agents or editors with additional and unnecessary work.

In addition, when agents and editors take proposals apart and copy them, pages can easily be lost. So number all proposal pages and, better yet, embed a header at the top of each page that identifies the project, the author(s), and lists some contact information. For instance:

PROPOSAL FOR WRITING BESTSELLING BOOK PROPOSALS   11/27/05
RICK FRISHMAN & ROBYN FREEDMAN SPIZMAN, 555-111-1212   -1-

Double-check all numbers in the index to be sure that they correspond to the correct pages on which each section begins. Also check that any page or section numbers that you refer to are accurate.

Submit everything in one neat package. Don't include any loose pages, photographs, or afterthoughts. Instead, attach them to a numbered page and place them in order in the proposal. Secure the entire package in a binder or with clips that can easily be removed. Send the entire proposal in a single box or container that gives it protection so that it will arrive in neat, crisp condition.

Some proposals are elaborate; they may include video or audiotapes of the author's presentations. Jennifer Enderlin, associate publisher at St. Martin's Press, said, "I've received proposals with candy, food, gifts, you name it. All that matters to me is the book itself."

Title Page

On the first or title page of the proposal, state:

(1) That this is a proposal for a book
(2) The book's title
(3) The book's subtitle
(4) "By"
(5) The author's name

For example:

A Proposal for the Book

Bestselling Book Proposals:
The Insider's Guide to Selling Your Work

By
Rick Frishman and Robyn Freedman Spizman

- Center all of the previous information.
- Call attention to both the title and subtitle by putting them in bold and italic type.
- Don't use colors or elaborate typefaces.
- If the author has a degree that is relevant to the book or his or her standing to write it, include it after the author's name.

Some writers like to include contact information after their names. If you decide to include it, limit it to your phone number and/or e-mail address. Adding your contact information will be unnecessary if you have inserted the header that we suggested above. However, if you prefer to give some contact information under your name, start the header on page 2, which will provide a cleaner look and eliminate duplication.

Agent John Willig doesn't believe that proposals should just be black and white and have coversheets with only the usual information. On the coversheet, he uses visuals and graphics, incorporates a capsule summary or a shortened elevator speech and gets into the author's marketing/publicity ability.

Willig wants to quickly show an editor that the proposal has qualities that they can sell. "It's a way to get and hold attention. The quicker you can get an editor to visualize a book, the closer you are to acceptance. When they say, 'I see this as a 5 by 8, in a bold style,' you know that you got through," Willig says.

Although visuals can help you grab an editor's attention, be careful not to send too many because the files you send can become huge. Sending huge files can overwhelm those who receive them and slow down or clog their systems.

Table of Contents and Sections

For nonfiction, a table of contents is not absolutely necessary, but it can help agents or editors quickly find specific proposal sections like

"Comparable Books," "About the Author," or "Promotion Plan." Since including a table of contents doesn't take much work and it can be helpful, we think including one is worthwhile. For fiction, a table of contents is necessary only when the entire manuscript has been submitted.

Center the table of contents and the pages on which each section begins. For instance:

Table of Contents

Overview	1
Comparable Books	3
Market for the Book	5
About the Author	7
Promotion Plan	8
Table of Contents	11
Summary of Chapters	12
Introduction	17
Sample Chapters	21
Press Clippings	45

Experts on proposal writing disagree as to whether each proposal section should begin on a separate page. We believe that the first section, the overview, should start immediately after the proposal table of contents and on the same page. However, we think that all subsequent sections should all start on a separate page in order to make it easier for agents and editors to read and copy individual sections.

Proposals can have different formats depending on the nature of the book. If you're in doubt, it's a good idea to run these details by your agent to determine his or her preference. Your proposal may have a few elements that vary from the standard ones; include the pieces that suit your book and will help it sell.

When you write your proposal, don't be redundant. Search thoroughly for words, phrases, and content that you repeated or overused and change them.

"When I write a book proposal, I always include all the basic pieces outlined earlier, but I also often include the following when I think it will help sell the book:

> A title page after the promotion plan to set up and separate the book content from the marketing information.

> On a few occasions, a cover page to communicate my book idea visually. Including a book cover is not generally recommended or required and can be costly. But when I was pitching visual books, more visual cover pages conveyed the true essence of the books and made the proposals look great.

> A full table of contents so that the agent can see the book at a glance, followed by a bulleted list of the content in each chapter or a summary of chapters.

> The introduction. Sometimes I refer to it as a 'Dear Reader' letter, but it could also be a preface. The intro sets the stage for the sample chapters that follow, and it's a critical element for nonfiction proposals. I work on the intro until it's so meaningful that there's nothing left to do but hopefully . . . buy that book!"

Some Author Do's for Proposals

If you have received endorsements for you and/or your book from instantly recognizable, big-name celebrities, authorities, or publications, insert the best one after the table of contents, just before the overview section. "Leading off with an endorsement only works if it's from a big celebrity. There is value in bringing celebrity to a project, but if it's gratuitous, it usually diminishes the project," agent Grace Freedson warns. "It's generally more important when you're writing cover copy for the book or to put a quote on the back."

Agents, editors, and editorial-board members think nationally, even globally. They won't be impressed by plaudits you receive from those they don't know. In fact, the opposite may be true: They may be turned off by the fact that those endorsers were the biggest names you could land, which could work against you.

On the other hand, some people feel that readers relate to endorsements from noncelebrities because they think that they're just like them.

If you provide an endorsement, indent it with two-inch margins from both sides. Keep the length to no more than three lines unless it's from Oprah, Katie, Kelly, Diane, Barbara . . . you get our drift! Set the quote in italic type enclosed by quotation marks. Give the name of the source in roman type directly below the quote and place it in the center or to the right side.

Carefully proofread your proposal at least twice to eliminate all typos, mistakes, and misspellings. Check all facts and figures. Consider hiring a professional editor to review your proposal; it could be a most prudent investment.

Some Author Don'ts for Proposals

Never send original artwork unless you have another, equally viable, copy. Artwork has an uncanny way of disappearing during the publishing process. So never submit artwork or materials that can't be replaced, without making special arrangements for them.

If possible, attach your name and contact information to all artwork you submit; keep copies and a list of what you submitted. Add captions for illustrations and check with your agent or editor on how many copies you should include.

Barring exceptional circumstances, your entire proposal (excluding sample chapters) should be in the twenty- to thirty-page range.

Action Steps

1. Write a practice cover letter. Identify any special information that should be included when you submit your proposal.
2. Who do you know? If you have a personal connection, highlight it in your cover letter.
3. Check your proposal format so it's simple to read and follow. Presentation is everything.
4. Remember not to include any valuable, one-of-a-kind item that you can't replace. If it's so rare and/or valuable, send a copy.
5. Look like the pros. Is your proposal ready, triple-checked, and flawless? Take the time to make sure that it looks great and that your editor's first impression of you as a potential author is a great one!

Remember:

▲ **A brief cover letter should accompany each book proposal to tell the reader what you sent.** A cover letter is not a second query. When you have a great platform, credentials, or media contacts, it may be worth mentioning. For example, if you are a doctor who appeared on *Oprah,* work it in.

▲ **Make the first page of the proposal the title page.** State that it is a proposal for a book, and give the book's title, subtitle, and your name as the author. Then provide a centered table of contents that lists the pages on which each section of the proposal begins. The first narrative section of the proposal should be the overview.

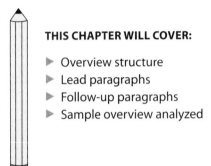

"Say all you have to say in the fewest possible words, or your reader will be sure to skip them; and in the plainest possible words or he will certainly misunderstand them."

John Ruskin

The Overview

THIS CHAPTER WILL COVER:

▶ Overview structure
▶ Lead paragraphs
▶ Follow-up paragraphs
▶ Sample overview analyzed

IN MANY WAYS, the route for getting books published parallels the path actors must follow to get theatrical or motion picture roles. In both fields, it all begins with, and builds on, progressively capturing the right people's attention.

A writer's query letter is equivalent to an actor's first audition, which is usually a "cattle call," where many hopefuls try out. A writer, on the basis of the quality of his or her initial query, may attract an agent's or editor's attention and be singled out from the rest of the pack. Like the actor who receives a callback and is invited to audition again, the writer may be asked to submit a proposal and may be given the opportunity to compete against more select, and often more experienced, candidates.

So there you stand, knees knocking, on that cold, drafty auditorium stage. As the director calls your name, it echoes through the building and you know that your time has come. You know that you have to open up with something dynamic, a powerful beginning that will launch you through this short-attention-span theater. Thank heavens you're prepared! Since you rehearsed and worked it through thousands of times, your initial lines come through loud and strong. You take an instant to listen—the theater is hushed, you hear only your own voice, it makes you feel great, so you press on.

While your book proposal and its overview section might not be so dramatic, they can be equally pivotal to your writing career. Agents and editors, like directors and producers, are busy people: They work under enormous pressures and endless demands. As a result, they have time only for those who can convince them right off the bat that they are special, that they can deliver something that no one else can.

Although most of the following is intended for proposals for non-fiction, much of it applies to fiction as well. A notable exception is the overview/synopsis. In a proposal for a work of fiction, submit a synopsis in place of the overview. As we previously discussed, some agents and editors want only a page or two whereas others will accept as many as five or six pages. Try to keep your synopsis brief, no more than two or three pages, which should be enough to demonstrate how clearly and concisely you can describe your book.

Overview Structure

The overview—which is also called the proposal introduction, summary, synopsis, or vision—is the first narrative section of your proposal. It's your first opportunity to roll out your artillery to sell your book. It also may be your only opportunity, so make it great, even greater than great!

The first thing most editors look at in a proposal is the overview. Their first question usually is, "What is the book about?" So, begin with a strong lead sentence that sets the tone and tells what your book is about. Show readers that you're a powerful force. Then, follow the lead with an explanatory sentence or two and as many well-organized and

Robyn Says

"Your book proposal is your opportunity; it's your demo or audition tape. It's your opportunity to stand alone at center stage under the spotlight and occupy an agent's or editor's complete attention, as brief as it may be. It's the time when you get to strut your stuff, to show the goods and make him or her beg for more. Your proposal gives you the chance to wow agents and editors with your exceptional book idea, its unlimited commercial potential, your brilliant writing talent, and your innovative promotional approach."

clearly written paragraphs as it takes to fully portray the virtues of the product you propose.

Structurally, an overview must contain a handful of mandatory ingredients. It must:

- Explain what your book is about.
- Distinguish your book from other books and explain why it is special.
- Identify your book's audience.
- State why you're qualified to write your book.

In addition, your overview should describe your book's format, organization, structure, themes, key elements or features, benefits, and conclusions. It should also detail the methods or approach you plan to take and when the book will be delivered.

Make Your Proposal Convincing

Agents and editors constantly receive tons of queries and proposals. Even though they specifically asked you to submit a proposal, they probably have little more than a vague memory of you or your book. Don't become lax because they sounded enthusiastic or delude yourself into thinking that you or your query made an indelible impression on them, because that isn't realistic.

Understand that it's incumbent upon you, from the start, to fully convince agents and editors that they should take you on. So, approach them as if you were starting from scratch, as if they were total strangers, and hit them with everything you have. When you submit your book proposal, it's better to repeat what you stated in earlier submissions or conversations than to let something major go unsaid.

Agent and book packager John Monteleone suggests that authors put their platforms up front. "The emphasis in publishing has changed. Publishers used to buy projects if they were well written and provided a good example of what was to come. Now, they immediately look to the author's platform. So it makes sense to put the author's platform up front. Publishers want to know who this person is who's writing this book, what opportunities does he or she bring for cross promotion, how great is his or her visibility, and how vigorously will he or she promote the book."

A book proposal must be structured. Since many editors have journalism backgrounds, they look for proposals that are written in the journalistic format. They want them to start with the following:

(1) A great title
(2) A great subtitle
(3) A great lead sentence

See Chapter 4 for our discussion of titles and subtitles.

When these three items are tight, it tells editors that you've thought through your book, its concept and how to best present it. It gives them reason to read further.

"An overview should tell an editor, in 50 to 100 words, (1) exactly what the book is, (2) why it's different from everything else, and (3) why you're the person to write it. Those are the three big things," according to Paula Munier, director of product development at Adams Media. "If writers don't get the hook right, the approach right, or the angle right, editors know that the book will probably be too generic for today's market."

Debra Englander, executive editor at John Wiley & Sons, Inc., wants an overview in one or two pages, "something that tells me what the book is, a snapshot of the book. A bit longer than an elevator pitch, but not much more."

"Structure your proposal so editors can get to the point in each section quickly," Jill Alexander, senior acquisitions editor at Adams Media suggests. "Think about prefacing important sections of the proposal with three key bullets. If you are one of only a few people certified in the country to do something, or the president of a 100,000-person organization that can buy lots of books, highlight those points with little sound bites that will grab the editor's attention and make him or her want to read on to learn more.

"Editors are notoriously overworked and simply inundated with correspondence," Alexander observes. "So do as much as you can to help them pick out essential information that will make them want to read more deeply. Using well-conceived, brief sound bites will also help them communicate the essence of your book to other editors and colleagues. Make it easy for them, don't make them dig through sixty or seventy pages of a proposal. Don't bury your lead." Even think about bulleting the main points in your query letter.

Referring to the Book in the Proposal

Work your book's full title into your lead paragraph and italicize it. Only include the subtitle if it's necessary to understand what the book is about.

When you refer to the title thereafter, two options exist—you can call it by:

(1) A shortened name; for example, after introducing *Writing Bestselling Book Proposals*, referring to it thereafter as *Proposals*. A nickname can personalize a book, make it sound less formal and reader-friendly. Don't use more than one nickname, which could be

confusing. In the overview, refer to the shorthand title at least once every third paragraph.

(2) Its title. If your book has a great title, think of it as your brand. Repeating your brand throughout the proposal will strengthen its identity with those who read it. In other proposal sections, initially give the full title. Then be consistent by following the usage you established in the overview.

Lead Paragraphs

The opening paragraph of the overview section should consist of a compelling lead sentence and one or two additional sentences that clarify, amplify, or build on the lead. After reading the first paragraph, readers should have a clear overall understanding of what your book is about and its target market. If you are a celebrity, state it up front in the lead paragraph.

Think of your lead paragraph as the introduction to the overview section, and your lead sentence as its headline. Actually, the lead should be more like an expanded headline, but don't make it too long. Try not to exceed two or so lines.

- Make your lead crisp, direct, and explosive.
- A lead sentence is not intended to tell the whole story; its job is to be the hook that grabs the reader and generates further interest.
- Capitalize on your lead by immediately following it with a sentence or two that provides additional or missing information.
- For optimum impact, try to keep your opening paragraph to no more than two or three sentences.

Lead sentences must be sculpted; they rarely come together the first few tries. Start by writing the first thing that comes to mind and then analyze each word to make sure it's necessary. If it's not, eliminate it. Then examine each remaining word and see if it most colorfully expresses what you want to say. Play around, substitute words, and write several versions. Your goal is to come up with a lead that describes your book, grabs readers' interest and compels them to read further.

Clarity is essential. Don't fall into the show-off trap. Many writers, especially novice writers, think that they must write witty, clever, or otherwise impressive lead sentences. Unfortunately, when most try, they fail to clearly describe their book. In a book proposal, clarity comes first; you must vividly describe your book so that readers have no question regarding what it's about. It's better to be rejected because agents or editors don't like your concept than because they don't understand it.

If you can be clear and also be clever and humorous, that's great, but consider it a bonus, not a mandatory requirement for your lead sentence. Don't risk obscuring or not adequately describing your book in order to show off; editors don't buy books from authors who don't write clearly.

The best way to start writing a lead sentence is to make a list of the key words or concepts you want to get across. Compiling a list will help you identify your book's strong points and those you want to emphasize, which is essential if you hope to clearly communicate them to agents and editors. It will also help you organize your thoughts. Don't try to write complete sentences; just jot down single words or short phrases.

Identify and number the three strongest points, those you want to stress in your proposal, and write a descriptive sentence about each. Place the three sentences in order and edit them to create a logical, coherent flow. Then, see if you can combine or merge any of your major points while still retaining the paragraph's impact and flow. If you can't, leave well enough alone. Finally, edit the entire paragraph by eliminating and replacing words.

If You Have a Hard Time Beginning

Writing lead sentences can be challenging for the most gifted and experienced writers. Some writers are never satisfied with what they compose, or they get blocked. When many encounter resistance, they become discouraged and quit. Don't let that happen to you!

When you can't write an acceptable lead sentence, try the following:

- Stop working on the lead and concentrate your effort on writing the rest of your overview. Then, when you've completed the overview, go back and try to write the lead again. Chances are that when you go back, you will be able to get it right, but if not, put it aside and sleep on it overnight. Don't look at it until the following day when you can approach it with fresh eyes and a less cluttered mind.
- Hone your skills by studying magazine, newspaper, and Web site headlines and advertisements.
  - Go to bookstores and leaf through magazines and periodicals.
  - Focus on the most descriptive, graphic, and expressive words and combinations of words.
  - Browse product sites on the Web. Web content is frequently set out in extended headline form; it runs a bit longer than the average headline and closer to what you need for lead sentences.
- Be direct. On occasion, all writers can be guilty of overdoing it when they try to impress and they don't express themselves well. Frequently, they concentrate more on being cute, witty, or sophisticated than on writing clearly. If that occurs, cut all the frills and get straight to the point. Simply write, "My book is about _____."
- Write a letter to a friend or relative in which you tell him or her about your book. Often, the mere fact that you're addressing a nonjudgmental reader will let you express yourself more easily. Ask the recipient whether he or she understands what your book is about and if he or she has any questions.

Questions, anecdotes, or quotes can also help you create powerful lead paragraphs. A good example is the quotation that Jay Conrad

Levinson and Michael W. McLaughlin used to start their proposal for *Guerrilla Marketing for Consultants* (John Wiley & Sons, 2004) and how they followed it up in their lead paragraph.

> *"If I never see one again, it will be too soon."*
> WILLIAM CLAY FORD JR., CHIEF EXECUTIVE, FORD MOTOR COMPANY

Mr. Ford was talking about consultants. His comment is enough to make even the most seasoned consultants wince. It is all the more ominous when one considers that his company "had no shortage of consultants" working on projects through the 1990s.

Another great example is Robyn's lead in the overview of her proposal for *Make It Memorable! An A–Z Guide to Making Any Gift, Event or Occasion . . . Dazzling!* (St. Martin's Griffin, 2004). Notice how Robyn asks three quick questions and then describes a problem in the lead paragraph. Then she offers the solution in a few follow-up lines.

> Have you ever attended a party that was so clever it had you talking for days? How about a dinner party that made you feel like royalty? Or, has someone done something so considerate and kind for you that it will be embedded in your heart forever? For some individuals, creating memorable moments comes easy, but for most, a little creative SOS provides welcome relief!
>
> Finally, here is a book that presents the ultimate resource for creating your own signature style . . . nothing less than unforgettable and memorable. Titled *Make It Memorable*, it's a one-stop shop for transforming your everyday style into round-the-clock memories.

Citing facts and statistics and giving opinions are great openings for proposal overviews. Asking questions and pointing out problems can be effective leads, but you must explain in a follow-up sentence how your book will provide the answer or solution.

Another great technique to use in the overview is to highlight the major attributes of your book with bullet points. Bullets immediately grab readers' attention and tell them about important information you want to drive home. Most professional proposal readers love bullet points because they lead them quickly to the heart of the writer's pitch.

When Bullets Work Best

Bulleted text should be written in short, headline-type sentences, preferably no longer than six or seven words. State the most important information, and if necessary, explain or amplify it later. Write no more than five to seven bulleted points; more can dilute the importance of all the bulleted information you provide.

Follow-Up Paragraphs

The remaining overview paragraphs should:

- Expand on your lead.
- Set forth the basic story your book will tell.
- Identify the audience that will find that story important.
- State why you are qualified to write it.
- Give the size and strength of your market.

Although your proposal will include a separate market-for-the-book section, the overview should foreshadow that section with at least one strong paragraph on your market's size and strength. Finish up by describing the format you propose, how you plan to proceed, and when the book will be delivered.

"Early in the overview, provide context on who is going to read the book and why. Then go into the content and structure of the book, how it's going to be put together, what kind of information will be included," book packager Leanne Chearney, of Amaranth, suggests. "Try to get the editor to see that you know what the book is, how it's going to be put together and what's going to go in it, because it increases the editor's confidence that you can deliver the book proposed. If you make a cogent argument as to who the audience is and who will be reading it, the editor can take it from there in-house.

"If you have a sidebar or a special feature that will run throughout the book, include an example of one in the overview, but don't exceed a paragraph or two," Chearney recommends. "Say that it will appear in every chapter, will cover this or that, will be approximately this length and here's one. You want the editor to see (1) what these features will look like and (2) that you know what they will look like. It will help show that you know how to execute your idea and that they won't have to do lots of editing."

If your book includes artwork, recipes, formulas, charts, checklists, or other similar items, insert examples of them in the text, or refer to them in the overview and provide samples of them at the end of the proposal. When you insert examples in the text, make sure that they're on the same page as the material discussed. Also position them so that they don't interrupt the flow of the editor's concentration on the text.

Special features can be set off, placed in boxes, or shaded to give them emphasis in the text. However, use these devices sparingly to

Rick Says

"Since publishing is so market-driven, define your audience as soon as possible. Even if you touched on it in the lead paragraph, drive it home in greater detail in the second and subsequent paragraphs. State specifically who will buy your book and why they will buy it.

"Identify your audience as narrowly as possible: married working women, single mothers with children, commuters, first-time home owners. Spell out what benefits your book will provide, how it will provide them and, if necessary, why those benefits are important."

avoid making your proposal gimmicky or fragmented. Editors can easily become confused or distracted by too many boxes or design elements, so keep them to a minimum. Usually, it's best to keep the look of your proposal as straightforward as possible and editorially consistent.

Think in terms of trends. "If you're a master gardener and you know that perennials are the big thing and you have a new idea regarding them, state specifically why the perennial trend is hot, how many people are doing it, and that you expect it to grow. It will show that you have a great idea and they you've really researched it and thought it through," Chearney adds.

Look what Levinson and McLaughlin did in a few paragraphs to define the market and the need for *Guerrilla Marketing for Consultants*. In their second proposal paragraph, they established that as we entered the new millennium, consulting was "a $127 billion global industry." But they point out that:

> . . . twenty years of learning from consultants and Internet-fueled changes in business have given rise to a new, more sophisticated breed of client like Mr. Ford, who is less satisfied with consultants, highly price sensitive, and less loyal. Fanning the flames of this buyer's market are the Enron debacle and subsequent corporate scandals that have intensified skepticism of consultants' credibility.

Then, the authors state that their book

> will be the first book to reveal how guerrilla marketing can transform today's challenges into a golden opportunity for winning *profitable* work from the new breed of consulting clients.

And, they round off their pitch by noting that their book will appeal to "more than five million readers with a personal or professional interest in consulting." Now that's a pretty strong sell!

Keep Your Focus

Agents and editors look for books that are narrowly focused. "The biggest mistake is trying to be all things to all people, when the focus isn't tight," literary agent Grace Freedson explains. "Your audience actually expands the tighter the focus of your proposal. For example, an author may think that the market for her children's book is ages four to fourteen, but four-year-olds want different books than fourteen-year-olds. You're better off more tightly defining your market. Your diet book may work for young adults, but not for others, and if you're job hunting, your strategy will differ depending on the state you're at in your career."

"It's really important for editors to be able to see the book," book packager Leanne Chearney notes. "I like to pepper proposals with excerpts or features that let them actually see that feature and how it will work. You should try to make editors see that you know what the book is, how it's going to be put together and what's going in it, because it increases their confidence that you can deliver the book you proposed."

Other important items that you should cover in the follow-up overview paragraphs include:

- That a noted authority or celebrity has agreed to write the foreword, preface, or introduction or to contribute in some way to your book.
- That your book will contain special features such as photographs, illustrations, charts, sidebars, forms, formulas, recipes, checklists, quizzes, action steps, or reference materials. When possible, state how many of these special features will be provided and identify the reference materials (recommended reading list, frequently asked questions, or resources). For even greater impact, attach examples of special features in an appendix to your proposal. However, don't forget our caution about submitting rare, valuable, or one-of-a-kind items that could be lost.
- How the completed book will be organized. For example, that it will contain a forward, introduction, and four sections, mak-

ing a total of twenty chapters and thirty pages of reference materials.

- A description of the content that will be provided and how it will be organized and written. Outline the format of the book, any special design features it will include and its overall look. Also describe the tone of the writing, whether it will be straightforward, easy to read, poetic, nontechnical, or humorous.
- The anticipated length, preferably the word count. Also mention how much has been written.
- When the book will be delivered and what resources you need to complete the book, if any. If artwork will be included in your book, say how you will deliver it.
- Special methods you will use to write the book. Will you compile and/or organize material written by others, rely on interviews, or interpret studies or statistics? If access to certain people or information is difficult, explain how you will gain it. When you have a subject that may be difficult to complete, explain your plan of attack in order to show the agent or editor that you have thoroughly thought through your approach.
- Special permissions you might need. For example, rights to use quotes, excerpts, visual, and other copyrighted material.

Although no firm rule of thumb exists, try to write an overview section that doesn't exceed three pages. Agents and editors have a lot to read, so saying your piece clearly and quickly could help your cause. Sure you have a lot of ground to cover, but understand that those who read your proposal will be looking for and impressed with authors who can express themselves in an economy of words.

Action Steps

1. Your overview is like a movie review. If it's great, you're likely to attract supporters. Elevate the great stuff to the top.

2. Think twenty-second sell. If after reading your overview for twenty seconds an editor is bored, he or she probably won't go any further. Make sure the twenty seconds the editor spends with your book are great!

3. Your overview is not the place to be shy, but don't be a braggart either. Promote yourself by citing measurable results: the number of years you've been at it, precise benefits you delivered and the amount of media coverage you've received.

4. Pay attention to every detail—spaces, margins, indents, and how you refer to your book—and be consistent. With editors, consistency really counts.

5. Refuse to be just a number. Do something that stands out without being gimmicky. Insert examples of special features, sidebars, charts, or diagrams. Design the cover or a logo for your book.

Remember:

⚠ **The first thing most editors look at in a proposal is the overview, and the first question they usually ask is, "What is this book about?"** The overview should quickly answer that question and convince the editor to read on. Begin the overview with a powerful lead sentence that sets the tone and demonstrates the writer's knowledge, skill, and professionalism.

⚠ **After the lead, the remaining paragraphs should expand on the lead, set forth the basic story the book will tell, and identify the audience that will benefit from the book.** You should also state why you are qualified to write the book and give the size and strength of the book's market. In addition, you should explain the format proposed, describe how you plan to proceed, and estimate when the book will be delivered.

chapter 10

"Publishing is such a copycat business. The trick is to stumble on a new trend or come up with something unique that has a market."

June Clark, agent, Peter Rubie Literary Agency

Comparative Analysis

THIS CHAPTER WILL COVER:

► The author's focus
► The purpose of comparative analysis
► Section format
► Taking a sharp focus
► Being better
► Sample analysis

AGENTS AND EDITORS want to know how your proposed book will differ from other similar books on the subject. Traditionally, experts on proposal writing have not stressed the importance of the comparable or competitive book analysis section to the extent that they emphasized other proposal sections, which we think is a major mistake. Sure, they all cover it and tell readers what to do, but most of them don't give it the same weight as the editors we interviewed do.

Frankly, we were surprised. The editors we interviewed for this book said, with virtual uniformity, that they placed great weight on the comparative analysis section and that it played a major role in their decision of whether to take on a writer. In most cases, it was the factor that they discussed most with us. Frequently, while we were discussing other points, they worked their way back to the subject of comparable books.

Since editors buy books, or at least champion them, we decided to follow their lead and give the comparative analysis section added prominence in this book. If this information is so important to editors, writers should give it to them quickly, right after the overview. It's a great way to impress them with your professionalism early in the proposal.

However, However, However

If the book is by a big celebrity, the celeb's bio should be the second section of the proposal. Place it immediately after the overview section and before the comparative analysis. Books by celebrity authors are driven more by the authors' celebrity than the topics of their books or other marketing factors. Capitalize on that celebrity prominently in the proposal because it will drive the book's marketability.

Hammer it home. If you're a celebrity, point it out in the lead paragraph of the overview section and expand upon it in follow-up overview paragraphs. Next, provide a star-focused biography as the second proposal section. Make yourself sound glamorous, well connected, and bigger than life, which is what most people want from celebrities. Agree to disclose insider stories about other celebs. Take bios that your publicist sends out and adapt them; make them juicy.

When editors look at a proposal, one of the main questions they ask is, "How is the book unique in the marketplace?" They want to know how it compares to the competition, so writers should list the high-profile books in their category. "If you can't tell us how your book is different, how can we tell someone else?" Kim Weiss, communications director for HCI Books, asks.

Knowing the competition is part of a writer's job. "When you have a good idea for a book, check other books before you put your proposal together, book packager Leanne Chearney suggests. "Check to see if your idea has been done, how well it's been done, and how you would do it differently. And while you're at it, see what publishers were involved, what editors, and how those books sold."

"Just listing the competitive books is no longer good enough," Roger Cooper, executive vice president of I Books, Inc., says. "Instead, writers should act as sort of an adjunct to the editor. Every editor thinks, 'What am I going to say in marketing and sales meetings and how much ammunition do I need?' For nonfiction books these days, editors need a huge amount of ammunition. The competitive breakdown helps editors because you've done a chunk of that work for them; it makes their lives easier.

"Writers should visit large chain booksellers and talk to the staff about which books, over the past six months, have been selling best in their category. They should find out if any particular book stands out and to what they attribute that success. Then, they should anecdotally state in the proposal that they went to two or three large book chains in a major city and the following are the books mentioned by the personnel at those stores as being the cream of the crop in their particular categories," Cooper advises.

According to booksellers Tim Hayes and Bonnie Bock, "Customers come into the store and ask us often how to get a book published. How do you get an agent? How do you promote a book? Is my idea viable? They'll pick up a bestselling book at our check-out counter and comment that they could have written that book, but of course, they didn't! However, just because we work at a bookstore, we don't have all the answers, but we can say what's flying out the door and who has the hottest diet book. A catchy title is critical and potential authors are smart to pay attention to the book marketplace."

While a comparative analysis section is a must in a proposal for nonfiction, it is usually not relevant for fictional works. By their very nature, works of fiction should be unique. Fiction editors know the market, and they're experts on what's been written, so they generally won't buy fiction that's already been done.

The Purposes

The comparative analysis section serves a number of important purposes. It should inform agents and editors of the following five points:

Point #1: *What Similar Books Exist*

Industry professionals constantly complain that proposals commonly state that, "no other books are like my book." With rare exceptions, agents and editors consider such statements total nonsense. Much of what authors write about was previously written. It may have been written with a different style, format or approach, but generally it's been written.

Many authors who see their work as unique are myopic. They feel that because their book takes a particular slant or direction, it stands alone. Agents and editors take a broader view. They see books in terms of topics or more generalized areas. They see a book sitting on a bookstore shelf with a bunch of other titles on the same or similar subjects.

Inaccurate representations in a proposal infuriate many agents and editors. They see it both as failure by writers to fully research the markets for their books and as a narrowness of vision that could undermine their work. When writers don't properly complete this major proposal section, many editors assume that they will not be up to the task of writing and promoting their books, which can be extremely hard and demanding work.

If, after conducting thorough research, you still believe that your book is unique, briefly discuss in your proposal some other books on the subject or on closely related subjects. Including this information will show agents and editors that you know the field and understand exactly where your book fits into the market.

Point #2: *How the Book Proposed Differs from Similar Titles*

Most agents and editors know the market, and if they don't, they can easily check what's in the marketplace. When the acquisition of a book is proposed in publishing houses, competitive books and the proposed book's niche are always discussed.

In many book proposals, the writers don't do a thorough or sophisticated job of distinguishing their books from others. Usually, it's clear that they haven't read or even looked at their book's competition. Often, they're simply paraphrasing self-serving Amazon.com reviews.

If you're serious about getting your book published, go to bookstores and spend time in front of the shelf where your book would be housed. Read, or at least leaf through, all of the nearby books that are similar or on the same general subject, to acquire a sense of how your subject has been treated. Check tables of contents and indexes to learn the content they provide and what they omit. Note competing books' formats, designs, special features, celebrity endorsements, and how their material is presented.

Check *Books In Print* (R. R. Bowker), which can be found in the reference section of your public library. Your agent and editor will. Also talk to your local public library staff and buyers and personnel at a well-stocked bookstore. Ask their opinions about competitive books, such as their strengths and weaknesses. Find out what buyers seem to like.

Visit Internet bookseller sites where you can see book covers and read online reviews. Frequently, you can access a book's table of contents and a sample chapter. Also note how many editions have been published. Check the books' sales ranks and whether the descriptions give their overall sales numbers. Sometimes a description will inform you, "35,000 copies sold." Internet bookseller sites also provide the names of similar and competitive titles that you can check out.

Distinguish your book by pointing out factors that set it apart from others like it:

- It takes a new or different slant or approach.
- It covers or stresses different facets of the subject.
- It is more comprehensive.
- It is more sharply focused.
- It is more business oriented.
- It takes a more humanistic approach.
- It is aimed at a different audience.
- It is based on newer information.
- It is less technical.
- It is easier to read.
- It is better illustrated.

Point #3: *That a Market Exists for the Proposed and Similar Books*

Some authors are reluctant to tell agents and editors that competitive or similar books exist. They have the erroneous impression that their book must be completely unique. As we've said, agents and editors know the market, and information about similar titles is easily found.

Providing information on similar books is beneficial to writers because it establishes that a market exists for the type of book they are proposing. If you can show a trend for books like yours or that sales of such titles have been traditionally strong, agents and publishers will show interest. Then, follow it up by explaining exactly where your book would fit into (a) the market and (b) publishers' lists or future plans.

To establish the market for your book, collect the sales figures for similar books. Some information is available on the Internet, either at booksellers' sites or from publishers' online catalogs. Ironically, publishers generally don't consider the sales figures posted in publishers' catalogs reliable. Many publishers rely on Nielsen BookScan (*www.bookscan.com*), a subscription service that electronically measures through-the-register sales at 4,500 U.S. book retail outlets and provides that information to subscribers via the Internet. It classifies sales into the following categories: adult fiction, adult nonfiction, children, and other. Within those categories, it further breaks down sales into groups including mystery, romance, art, and cooking. BookScan caters to the publishing industry and not the general public.

For some additional punch, also include the names of all magazines and newsletters on your book's subject in the comparative analysis section. List the circulation figures for each of these publications in order to demonstrate the broadness of the market. A lot of circulation information can be obtained via the Internet or at libraries.

Point #4: *That the Writer Understands His or Her Book's Niche*

Since the competition for the readers' dollars is so intense, agents and editors want assurances that writers are focused on reaching viable markets. From experience, they know that writers who understand how their books fit into the market will usually write and promote their books more successfully.

"An author who understands where his or her book fits is a total asset," Danielle Chiotti, acquisitions editor at Adams Media, explains. "My most successful authors are the ones with the clearest visions. They understand who their competitors are and what their market is."

As an authority, you are expected to know your field inside out. It's your job to know what's happening in your area and where your book will fit. "A writer writing a book should own or have read every book on the subject," Diane Reverand, editor at St. Martin's Press, declares. Authors must know what books will be sitting next to theirs on bookshelves and how their books differ. To create the most successful works, they should know the strong points of other books as well as their weaknesses. Then they can zero in on their own particular niche and write better books or attract different readers than their neighbors and competitors do.

Point #5: *That the Writer Has Done His or Her Homework*

The fact that writers are familiar with similar books on their subjects provides a strong indication that they will perform well and be good for agents and editors to work with. Since so much money is on the line in publishing, agents and editors tend to have heightened sensitivities, which are predominantly ruled by the bottom line. Agents and editors often interpret the most miniscule signs, signs that you and your colleagues might never notice, as indications that an author can't or won't produce or will be trouble. Since editors have enough on their plates without taking on "difficult" writers, they generally pass on them.

In the publishing business, disaster stories circulate like bestsellers, and they have long shelf lives. Since no one likes to be burned, protective measures have taken root.

Although most good editors check the competition themselves, writers who provide a thorough competitive analysis give themselves a psychological positive. It shows editors that they have authors who are thinking as marketers, not just as writers, which is what editors and publishers want—authors who will be marketing partners.

"Some writers have told us that they resent the fact that agents and editors expect them to do comparable book analysis. They think that it's part of the agent's or editor's job, and that the writer's job is to write the book. They also feel that agents and editors are better suited to this task because they're familiar with the market, know books, and have research materials in-house.

"Well, if that's how you feel, get realistic and adjust your attitude. Publishing has changed. With consolidation, fewer people are doing more work; everyone is spread too thin. Writers are now expected to research comparable books. It's part of their due diligence, to steal an overused business-school term. Simply put, today, reporting on the competition is part of an aspiring author's job, like it or not!

"Clearly showing how your book differs from others and pointing out where it's better are great ways to impress agents and editors. It could be instrumental in convincing them to take on your book."

All good editors will check with their salespeople, with Amazon.com and BookScan, but if seven or eight competitive books are listed in a proposal, a busy editor may check only the first two or three. If the writer's analysis checks out, the editor may feel more assured that the author has provided accurate information on the remaining competitors; some may even accept what the writer submits.

When writers submit materials that editors can rely on, trust is built. Such trust often becomes the basis for a good, successful, and long-running editor-writer relationship.

Format

In this section, provide an annotated list of all competitive and comparable books that are still in print. Don't overwhelm agents and editors with a list of every book ever published on the subject, but make sure you cover all the leading titles with which they might be familiar.

Are any bestsellers? If so, place them and other well-known books first. If your book is in the academic, scholarly, or intellectual realms, give prominence to those that have received critical praise from authorities in their fields. Start by listing the full title of each comparable book in italics. Then, in roman type, state the author's name, publisher's name, year published, number of pages, and cover price. Finally, if you have sales figures, include them. Including sales figures should impress agents and editors because they know that sales information is hard for writers to obtain. For example:

> *In the Main: Reflections from the Middle,* by Brian Feinblum (FS Press, 2002, 224 pp., $14.95, 17,500 copies sold).

Agent Sharlene Martin instructs her clients to include images of the covers of the comparable books they discuss. This embeds a strong visual representation in an editor's mind, looks great, and shows the agent that her clients are creative and think out of the box, which is most appetizing to editors.

Sharpen Your Focus

Agents and editors want sharply directed and narrowly focused books, but writers usually try to take a wider focus because they think it will bring their books more sales. It's imperative that authors do their homework and identify their competition. If they research the competition and find six books similar to theirs, they can shape their books for new and untapped audiences.

Writers have a distinct advantage over other businesspeople; it's easy for them to learn about the competition . . . all they have to do is buy their competitor's books. Only by examining their books can you learn how they're structured, the content they provide, what they include, and what they leave out. After you review the competition, you can determine what you can do better, what else you could include, and the approaches you can take to distinguish your book.

Knowing the competition will show you how to differentiate your book and find a niche that other writers have not exploited. For example, instead of writing another diabetic cookbook, you could decide to write a cookbook for diabetics who miss eating dessert, who are pregnant, or who want to participate in physically demanding sports. Rather than writing a book about relationships in general, your research might convince you to do a volume on relationships for single mothers, for families with two working parents, or for families with racially mixed children.

A sharp focus doesn't narrow your audience; it just defines your audience more clearly, which is what editors and agents want. Instead of doing a broad book on infidelity, write a book on the type of people who are unfaithful, young women who are unfaithful, wives who are being cheated on, or the other women.

To clarify your focus, talk to avid readers. Question people in bookstores and gift stores; get in the know. Find out if your category is a big seller and if not, what it would take to make it so. Ask booksellers if customers ask for books on your topic. If so, what books do they recommend?

Show Why You're Better

When you identify books most like yours, distinguish your book. Show how the books differ and how yours will be better. Explain if it will be better for a particular or a new audience. Since the major purpose of your proposal is to sell your book, sing its praises. However, in doing so, be honest, fair, and avoid hype.

■ Truthfully point out the competition's weaknesses, but don't be petty or nitpick.

"In the comparable analysis section of the proposal for *Good Behavior*, my coauthors, Drs. Garber and Garber, and I addressed how other bestselling parenting books discussed a specific technique to curb children from climbing out of their beds. In our proposal, we pointed out that several of those titles advocated outdated behavioral strategies. In the proposal for *Good Behavior*, we emphasized that we had a 'new and improved' approach, which demonstrated the need for an updated book on the subject. The proposal created a bidding war that produced multiple offers, and we selected Villard, an imprint at Random House, as our publisher."

- Don't disparage the competition. Instead, stress elements that your book includes that competitive books lack.
- Give praise where it's due and state how you will incorporate outstanding features of competitors' books in your work.

Throughout the comparative analysis section, remember that your primary job is to convince agents and editors that a market for your book exists, not to annihilate the competition. So, clearly point out the unique features that will compel readers to buy your book, rather than bash your competitors.

Sample Analysis

The competitive analysis in the proposal for Rick and Steven Schragis's book, *10 Clowns Don't Make a Circus,* takes a unique and creative approach. In an introductory paragraph, the authors state that similar books in their genre, general all-purpose business guides, are consistent bestsellers. Then they describe five outstanding books in the category and spell out the advantages of their proposed book. Their analysis is provided on the next page.

Positioning *10 Clowns Don't Make a Circus* vs. Recent Business Books

General all-purpose business advice guides are consistently bestsellers, year after year. Many millions of people already in the business world want to do better, either by getting ahead or by going into business for themselves. It's certainly true that "knowledge is power"—thus the persistent and strong demand for concise "on the money" advice on how to manage people, schedules, teams, negotiations, typical pitfalls, and challenges, etc.

***Never Confuse a Memo with Reality: And Other Business Lessons Too Simple Not to Know* by Richard A. Moran (HarperBusiness, 2002, 160 pp., $9.00).**
Moran, the National Director of Organization Change Practice for Price Waterhouse, has distilled the business world into a collection of 355 aphorisms that have a lighthearted tone somewhat similar to that of the series of *Dilbert* books. Typical advice includes:

- Never take a newspaper to the bathroom.
- Never tell a colleague he looks tired.
- Never in your life utter the phrase "It's not my job."

The *10 Clowns Don't Make a Circus* Advantage

Moran's observations are all one-liners, and as one reviewer has observed, "Sometimes it's difficult to explain why these statements are true." The rules in *10 Clowns Don't Make a Circus* are clearly explained and often augmented with tips for how to achieve or follow them.

***Good to Great: Why Some Companies Make the Leap . . . and Others Don't* by Jim Collins (HarperBusiness, 2001, 320 pp., $27.50).**
Author Jim Collins and his team of researchers put together this bestseller by sorting through a list of over 1,000 companies, looking for those that made substantial improvements in their performance over time. They finally settled on eleven and discovered common traits that challenged many of the conventional notions of corporate success. The book

offers detailed and insightful advice, but only based on the eleven companies chosen. Seems primarily aimed at senior executives of very large companies.

The *10 Clowns Don't Make a Circus* Advantage

Good to Great is highly research based, which gives it first-rate academic credentials, but it may be too dry and sophisticated to qualify as a popular advice book. In other words, it aims above the heads of most middle managers or potential entrepreneurs.

The Daily Drucker: 366 Days of Insight and Motivation for Getting the Right Things Done by Peter F. Drucker with Joseph A. Maciariello (HarperBusiness, 2004, 488 pp., $27.95).

Revered management thinker Peter F. Drucker has often been called the original management guru. This thoughtful day-by-day companion offers his penetrating and practical wisdom on everything from time management and organization to innovation and outsourcing. It provides useful insights for each day of the year.

The *10 Clowns Don't Make a Circus* Advantage

These 366 daily readings are an excellent compendium of Drucker's voluminous output of books and articles—but it's all Drucker, every single page. *10 Clowns Don't Make a Circus* provides the best thinking of many experts, from all areas of business. Drucker's stellar reputation is well deserved, but his writing style is professorial and cumbersome—best for the MBA crowd.

You're Hired: How to Succeed in Business and Life from the Winner of The Apprentice by Bill Rancic (HarperBusiness, 2004, 208 pp., $22.95)

From the winner of the popular TV reality show *The Apprentice,* in which Donald Trump (who provides a foreword) slowly eliminated potential personal assistants until only Rancic was left standing. *You're Hired* is more about Rancic, the strategy he used to win and a behind-the-scenes look at his *Apprentice* experience, than a conventional guide to business success.

The *10 Clowns Don't Make a Circus* Advantage

While *You're Hired* offers some tidbits of business wisdom and a taste of Bill Rancic's dynamic entrepreneurial philosophy, its main purpose isn't really to present or explain essential business rules—and it certainly does not do so in any comprehensive or systematic fashion. The talented author clearly outlines what it takes to satisfy "the Donald"—but provides little insight beyond that.

First, Break All the Rules: What the World's Greatest Managers Do Differently by Marcus Buckingham and Curt Coffman (Simon & Schuster, 1999, 255 pp., $28.00).

Two consultants for the Gallup Organization debunk some beloved management myths such as "Treat people as you like to be treated," "People are capable of almost anything," and "A manager's role is diminishing in today's economy." Culling their observations from more than 80,000 interviews conducted by Gallup during the past twenty-five years, the authors outline the key to becoming an excellent manager.

The *10 Clowns Don't Make a Circus* Advantage

More than any of the previous books mentioned, *First, Break All the Rules* does offer helpful advice on how to become a more effective manager. But the authors primarily shatter common misconceptions—in other words, explaining what doesn't work. While there is certainly value to be gained by avoiding other managers' mistakes, the *10 Clowns Don't Make a Circus* approach is more practical, straightforward, and positive.

Action Steps

1. Visit bookstores. Go to the shelf where your book would be placed and get to know its neighbors. Read and review competitive and comparable books.
2. Decide how your book differs and is better than similar books. Establish a case for your book that will show a publisher why readers will buy it.

3. When possible, research how many books the bestselling book in your category sold and collect any and all facts or statistics that support your book.
4. Explain exactly what makes your book better. Establish a unique selling proposition based around your book's advantages.
5. Think of your book as if it were running for office. What makes it the best candidate compared to other books? If it's first in a category, say so. If it's not first, make sure it's the best.

Remember:

⚠ **When editors receive a proposal, one of their main questions is, "How is this book unique in the marketplace?"** They want to know how the book compares to the competition, so list and compare the high-profile books in your book's category. Describe the other books and distinguish your book from them. When possible, state why your book is better.

⚠ **Knowing the competition is part of a writer's job.** If you present yourself as an authority, you must know your field of expertise inside and out, including what everyone else in the field has written. Act as an adjunct to your editor and give him or her ammunition to distinguish your book from the competition in marketing and sales meetings. The publisher's sales team can then use those distinctions to convince wholesalers and retailers to stock your book. Comparative analysis helps identify the markets for proposed books.

CHAPTER

11

"You must keep sending work out; you must never let a manuscript do nothing but eat its head off in a drawer. You send that work out again and again, while you're working on another one. If you have talent, you will receive some measure of success—but only if you persist."

Isaac Asimov

Markets for the Book

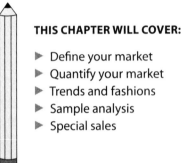

THIS CHAPTER WILL COVER:

▶ Define your market
▶ Quantify your market
▶ Trends and fashions
▶ Sample analysis
▶ Special sales

WRITERS FREQUENTLY CAN'T SEE beyond their own excitement and involvement in their books. They often think that their book ideas are so great, so earthshattering, and so universal that publishers will stand in line to bid for them. Writers' passions can blind them. They may cause them to totally overlook the realities of publishing, the fact that publishing is a business, and that in order to get their books published, they have to convince agents and publishers that their books will appeal to a substantial audience.

Agents and editors tell us that writers commonly make outlandish, unsubstantiated claims such as, "My book will be bigger than the Bible," "It will outsell *Tuesdays with Morrie*," or "The film rights alone will make it unnecessary for my grandchildren to ever work." Such wild claims turn off agents and editors and may help them decide not to take on these books.

Writers should be intimately familiar with their markets. Before they even approach an agent or editor, they should know exactly:

- What readers their book addresses.
- Why those people need their books.
- How readers will benefit from their books.

It's an investigation that every aspiring author should undertake, but unfortunately, that's not the way it works. Most of the time, writers have a weak grasp of their market; they frequently don't know how to define it.

"Sometimes you have a great idea, but you have to find your voice," author Stedman Graham explains. "You have to make a connection to the reader and the need in the marketplace that you are targeting. Who is your target market and how do you make a connection with the marketplace? The work of an author should be representative of the person writing the material. It's all about authenticity. That's the only thing that will overcome the obstacles that you'll face in writing the book and then marketing it.

"You have to believe in it, since you'll have a lot of doubt with the topic. They'll ask, 'Who are you?' And if you don't believe in yourself, then you can't last throughout the scrutiny. You have to be a leader to write a book since it's a leadership position. You are telling other people what to do. It's a position of authority, so you become a target for criticism," Graham says.

In this chapter, we're going to tell you how to define your book's greatest possible market and also convince your prospective publisher that you are the person who can reach it.

Define Your Market

Before people go into business, it's essential for them to define their market. They must know who their customers will be—who will buy

"It's very important for writers to define their audience early in the game before they get too deeply involved in the writing. By examining their audience and who will buy their book up front, they may find that their book lacks large enough potential markets or that they have been addressing a small, select, or noncommercial group. If it's still early in the process, they can change or adjust their direction, write for a larger or more focused audience and increase their book's appeal.

"Consider not only the magnitude of your audience, but also how easy it will be for your book and message to reach it. For example, larger audiences frequently can be reached through their business associations or similar organizations."

their goods and services and provide them with the income that will enable them to operate. It's simply the way business works.

Aspiring writers, whether they write fiction or nonfiction, must ask the same question. Who will their customers be, who will buy their books, who will pay for what they offer for sale? Knowing these answers will help them to write and promote their books.

Frequently, the answer is apparent—you wrote your parenting book for readers with preteen children, or your vegetarian cookbook for those on low-fat diets. In such cases, try to identify additional markets, other groups that would buy your book. Come up with as many as you can, but be reasonable and don't stretch the truth. For example, teachers, group leaders, and coaches might also need your parenting book.

In some cases, the target audiences for certain books won't be as clear. Authors often write their books more for themselves, not for others. They may need to work through problems, develop deeper understandings, boost their careers, or simply express themselves.

If you write fiction, briefly identify the market for your book in your proposal's synopsis, after you describe your book. Just mention it. However, if you write nonfiction, provide more.

Here's what to do:

1. Identify your core market; state who will be the primary buyers of your book. List them according to their similarity of interests, problems, businesses and careers, age, sex, families, beliefs, and so on. Be specific and quantify the size of the group and explain how your book uniquely meets their needs. (See the next section, "Be Factual," in which we discuss how to quantify your market.) List and discuss your largest market first.

    If you're writing a book on adverse reactions from eating peanuts, your core readers will be those who suffer from peanut allergies, their families, health workers, teachers, and caregivers. Since about 3 million Americans suffer from peanut or tree-nut allergies, it's reasonable to project a reader base somewhere in excess of 3 million people, which is not a bad start.

    Explain that your book will save lives by teaching readers how to identify foods and recipes that may contain hidden or unsuspected peanuts or tree nuts. State that it will instruct readers exactly what to do when these items are eaten or at the first sign of a reaction. Name the medicines that should be carried at all times, provide instructions on administering them, and tell what, precisely, to do if they're not on hand.

2. Then, identify and define your secondary or crossover markets. How many health practitioners specialize in treating food allergies? What is the number of medical schools and medical and health libraries?

3. After you identify and quantify your reader base, get creative. Explore how you can expand your reader base or develop other marketing opportunities such as spin-offs and products. Ask yourself who else might be interested in a book on peanut allergies, and what do they have in common and how can you reach them. Would it be worthwhile to shape or market your book to reach them? Would your book be of value to those who have other allergies?

4. Also explore products that you could develop to expand your market. For instance, warning bracelets or jewelry, and laminated cards listing surprising foods that contain peanuts, peanut oil, or peanut butter. Perhaps you could arrange bulk purchases or tie-ins with pharmaceutical companies, food companies, restaurant associations, or health-care providers.

Be Factual

Don't exaggerate or make wild, unrealistic claims about your book's prospects or potential sales. Although it's important to be enthusiastic, to believe in your work and to pursue your dreams, it's imperative to face reality. Understand that the book industry is market driven, and if you want to get published, you must present information about your book in a way that will make publishers willing to buy it. This requires you to do your homework—to identify your audience and its size and to explain why it's going to buy your book.

Claiming that your book will attract a huge audience simply isn't enough; you must substantiate your claims. Making wild, undocumented claims is a sure way to turn off agents and editors. They want facts and figures. The editorial boards that ultimately approve book acquisitions are bottom-line oriented. If they don't think a book will make the house money, they usually won't agree to buy it. So as the author, it's up to you to show them in black and white that buying your book will be a great financial move.

Many authors believe that it's the publisher's job to justify the market, and to some degree that may be true. Few publishers invest without first fully running the numbers, and they will definitely verify your claims. However, since you, the writer, have so much riding on your proposal, present your own best case. Point the number crunchers in the right direction; show them that you've done your homework and that you're a professional. Plus, you may come up with an angle, an approach or something new that they may not have considered.

Defining Your Market in Detail

Build and expand on the discussion of the market for your book that you included in the overview section. Quantify the size of the specific groups and demographics that you identified as those most likely to buy your book, and state the buying power of each. Describe your market in terms of:

- Statistics, facts, and figures on who will buy your book, why they will buy it, and the amount of money that is annually spent in each market.
- List how your audience gets information from sources such as magazines, radio, TV, cable, and Internet sites. Specifically name what they read, listen to, watch, and browse. Provide the circulation or viewership numbers for each source.
- Outline what the members of your market do, their jobs, duties, hobbies, and interests. State where they vacation, travel or go for entertainment, health, and conditioning, or for stimulation or relaxation.
- If they will buy your book in some special or unique way such as through schools; businesses; and religious, community, or charitable organizations; state how and explain why.

To obtain hard data for your proposal, conduct research via the Internet and at libraries. Check your subject matter and everything related to it on Google and other search engines. Also research online booksellers.

The government, specifically the Department of Labor, is a great source for figures, trends, and statistics. So are industry and trade associations. Indexes of trade and industry associations can be found on the Internet by checking such sites such as *http://dir.yahoo.com/Business_and_Economy/Organizations/Trade_Associations* and *www.marketingsource.com/associations*.

Most industry and trade associations put out publications that are loaded with helpful statistics and projections. They usually report

the number of people the industry serves and the size of the market. You may also find great articles on trends and wonderful quotes. Some of these publications, or portions of them, are online. Other helpful industry and trade information can be found on associations' Web sites. Make sure to check news, publicity, and pressroom sections.

Regularly read these publications and clip out items with information that you could include in your proposal. In addition, check these publications' archives to see if any of them have published articles on your book's subject. If so, get copies and attach them to your proposal. Articles from such sources will give your book's champion powerful information to take to the board.

Also speak with people in your field(s) of interest. Find out what publications they read and how they get information on their businesses, careers, interests, hobbies, etc. See which of those sources are online and how you can access the others. Ask them to put you in touch with knowledgeable people in their fields.

Trends and Fashions

Publishing follows the media. Usually, the media stirs up interest and a trend develops. Then publishers rush to issue books that explain and examine those trends or tell readers how to make money from them. In your proposal, seize upon hot topics, the latest rages. Latch on to them and point out how your book relates to them; use the momentum of trends to launch your project. Emphasize that your book is timely, important, and unique, that it will neatly dovetail with the current rage and make lots of money for the publisher.

Being the first to the market can be a windfall for publishers. So, if your book will be the first, state it clearly. However, don't claim to be the first if you're not or may not be when your book comes out. Understand that other publishers will also be trying to capitalize on the trend and may be able to beat you and your publisher to the market.

When possible, cite statistics or monetary figures to show the growth of trends. For example, from 1999 to 2005, the sales of cellular-telephone attachments have increased by 10 percent annually.

Remember, if you can't be first, you can at least be best!

Sample Analysis

Now let's examine Levinson and McLaughlin's proposal for *Guerrilla Marketing for Consultants*, which includes an outstanding example of a section describing markets for the book. In their proposal, the authors thoroughly analyzed the potential markets for *GMC*, broke them down in segments and provided verifiable statistics to justify the size of the various audiences their book could attract.

Note how Levinson and McLaughlin identified their potential market. First, they began with the largest segment of their overall audience and then they divided it into smaller groups. McLaughlin's connection and ready access to a network of 75,000 members of Deloitte firms are also prominently stressed.

Guerrilla Marketing for Consultants will appeal to more than 5 million potential readers:

▶ A powerful, attention-grabbing section opener in which the authors quantify the size of their potential market.

Consultants and Consulting Firms

Management consultants are a significant audience for *GMC*. In April 2002, the Bureau of Labor Statistics estimated that nearly 500,000 professionals were employed in management consulting services. The 2002 edition of *Consultants and Consulting Organizations Directory* profiles more than 25,000 consultancies in the United States and Canada, ranging in size from solo practitioners to firms with 11,000 consultants in hundreds of branch offices.

▶ Here the authors follow up their strong, but general, lead sentence by defining their primary market—management consultants—and documenting its size.

As a partner with Deloitte Consulting, Michael McLaughlin has ready access to the network of 75,000 partners and professionals at Deloitte Consulting and the allied firm of Deloitte & Touche. Deloitte has offices in every major market and serves the world's largest companies.

▶ McLaughlin's special broad network access as a Deloitte partner is stressed.

GMC will appeal to consultants in small, medium, and large firms, including new and veteran practitioners, as well as leaders of consulting firms. The book will also be relevant for internal consultants, those who provide consulting services within large companies like Shell Oil and in government agencies and educational institutions.

Consultants Abroad (in English)

Management consulting is a global profession with hundreds of thousands of members abroad. The International Council of Management Consulting alone represents thirty-three foreign countries with multiple consulting organizations in each country. Consultants in foreign countries, most of whom are fluent in English, will be interested in the guerrilla message and methods, especially in Canada, Great Britain, Australia, Japan, the Netherlands, and Germany.

▶ These paragraphs expand the scope of the authors' market to show that their book will appeal to consultants in firms of all sizes and globally.

Professional Services Providers

Other experts who offer professional services to clients are another substantial market for the book. More than three million Americans are consultants in areas such as: engineering, law, accounting, architecture, banking, financial and investment counseling, public relations, independent contracting, urban and environmental planning, human resources, health care, professional speaking, executive training and coaching, corporate learning, and interior design.

Consulting and Professional Associations

Another market for the book will be the organizations and associations that maintain library resources for consultants and other professional services providers, such as the Association of Management Consulting Firms, National Speakers Association, Association of Professional Consultants, Association of Executive Search Consultants, Institute of Management Consultants, American Management Association, and the Society of Telecommunications Consultants.

▶ The authors further expand the market for their book by pointing out additional markets. They quantify that 3 million experts provide consulting services and name some of the groups that maintain libraries that can buy their book.

Business Students and Educators

Business schools provide additional marketing opportunities for *GMC*. *BizEd*, the magazine of the Association to Advance Collegiate Schools of Business, claims an audience of nearly 2 million business students worldwide. *Business Week Online*, in its 2001 "The Best Business Schools" report, profiled the 250 best business programs. These 250 schools reported enrollment of 500,000 business students (200,000 graduate and 300,000 undergraduate).

The 2002 Universum graduate and undergraduate business school surveys point to a significant interest in consulting among business students. According to the MBA survey, "Management consulting is easily the industry that MBA students would most often like to join, having grown in popularity since last year from 19 percent to 30 percent." The undergraduate survey shows that even more undergraduate business students, 36 percent, would ideally like to work in management consulting. The content and style of *Guerrilla Marketing for Consultants* will appeal to aspiring consultants and to those headed into other professional services careers.

The thousands of people who provide graduate and under-graduate business education will also be audiences for the book, including business school deans, department chairs, program directors, faculty members, librarians, as well as academic and career counselors. The book will lend itself to adoption in business-school curricula in areas such as marketing, management, and entrepreneurship.

▶ The authors discuss the educational market and the fact that it has 2 million business students. They point out the popularity of management consulting with students and that their book can also be used for teaching.

Consulting Clients

The book will help clients and potential clients better understand what they can and should expect from consultants. In particular, those with the responsibility for purchasing consulting services, such as CEOs and CIOs, will be a market for the book.

Libraries

GMC will be attractive to libraries because of its place in the *Guerrilla Marketing* series of books, and because of its usefulness as a reference. In addition to business-school collections, library markets for the book include public, corporate, and government libraries.

▶ Finally, the authors explain how their book will help management-consulting clients and be a staple in business libraries.

Special Sales

Special sales, which are the selling of books outside the traditional bookstore channels, have become a huge and growing market for books. Giant retailers such as Target, Wal-Mart, and Home Depot are enormous outlets for books. Selling your book *Mitering for Morons* at Home Depot alone could generate huge sales.

Visit retail outlets and note the types of books they sell. The liquor store downtown could be an ideal place for your book on the history of bourbon, and Starbucks could really sell lots of your espresso book.

Don't forget libraries; library sales can certainly help your book. In addition to the sales themselves, the presence of your book in libraries gives it great visibility, and readers who like it may decide that it's a title they want to own, give, or recommend.

The library market is not limited to public libraries. Schools, businesses, hospitals, courts, and other institutions also have extensive libraries where your book might fit.

Warning: Certain libraries and institutions are reluctant to purchase workbooks or books in which readers are requested to write answers. They don't want their books marked up because they feel it makes the books less desirable for subsequent readers.

Although foreign translations are technically not special sales, they are closely related. Many books easily lend themselves to different languages and cultures whereas others never really work. Explore the prospect of selling your book abroad. Your title on how to run your own publicity campaign could appeal to huge audiences in countries with emerging markets.

Some books also work well in the audio or spoken format or as instructional videos. If these approaches would be ideal for your project, stress it in your proposal.

Action Steps

1. *Define your market.* Who will buy your book? Make sure you know exactly who your buyers will be and the specific audiences that will become supporters and readers.
2. *Find statistics on the number of people who could be buyers of your book.* Giving numbers stresses the size of your potential audience and can convince publishers that your book could be a big seller.
3. *Point out trends that illustrate why this is such a timely book.* It is your job to prove both the need for and the appeal of your book. Publishers may not be aware of certain trends, so don't assume that they are.
4. *Identify special sales that could be developed for your book.* Explore what other audiences, companies, and groups might be interested in buying multiple copies or customized editions of your book.
5. *Consider your book a business.* Know who will want it and the different markets it will reach. The more markets your book can reach, the greater its sales potential.

Remember:

 State in your proposal who your audience is. Precisely identify the demographic groups that will buy your book by pointing out their common interests, problems, businesses and careers, ages, sex, families, beliefs, and so on. Quantify the size of those groups and explain the benefits they will obtain. List and discuss the largest markets first.

 Don't exaggerate or make unrealistic claims about your book's prospects or potential sales. Although it's important to be enthusiastic and believe in your work, it's equally important to show your professionalism and reliability by providing factual information that editors can verify and use to sell the project to their boards.

"The reserve of modern assertions is sometimes pushed to extremes, in which the fear of being contradicted leads the writer to strip himself of almost all sense and meaning."
Winston Churchill

About the Author

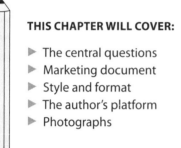

THIS CHAPTER WILL COVER:

► The central questions
► Marketing document
► Style and format
► The author's platform
► Photographs

IN THIS PROPOSAL SECTION, writers have the opportunity to blow their own horn, to state why they're so ideally qualified to author their book. Agents and editors are consistently amazed that so many are far off-key.

"I want to know about the writer," New York City agent June Clark tells us. "Many don't tell me anything about their backgrounds and credentials. Some, who don't have credentials, deliberately leave them out for fear of being rejected. But just as many others, who have amazing credentials, are just modest or don't seem to be impressed by their own accomplishments. The people who blow their own horn are always the ones who don't have the credentials. The ones who have tremendous knowledge and experience in their fields tend to take that knowledge for granted. They say, 'Oh, it's no big deal,' because they're in a universe with people who are brilliant and may have even more impressive credentials."

The Central Questions

When agents and editors receive a proposal, they wonder, "Can the author actually write this book; can he or she complete it?" "Does the author have the qualifications to write it and will he or she deliver and energetically promote a first-rate book that will sell?"

Every publishing venture is a risk. Questions exist about even the most well-known and successful authors. Unforeseen problems arise and torpedo books that seem to be rock solid, absolute sure things. Murphy's Law, which holds that whatever can go wrong will go wrong, has an uncanny way of surfacing at the strangest times.

So, to reduce their risks, editors and publishers search for information—any little facts, tidbits, or indications—that can help them make more enlightened acquisition decisions. The information you provide about yourself is not taken lightly; it can go a long way in helping publishing professionals make decisions that can change your career.

Marketing Document

A deadly mistake many writers make is simply including their basic, tired old resumes in their book proposals. In most cases, they dig them out from deep in a drawer, where they may have been sitting forever. Then they update here and tailor there and essentially adapt what they've already got on hand.

The inclusion of your biography in your proposal is not a formality; it will not just be quickly scanned and then buried forever in an editor's file. The biography provides essential information that goes to the heart of a book proposal. It may be the clincher that determines whether you get a book deal or not.

Start from scratch. Use your old resume as nothing more than a reference document to check names and dates. Write the biography for your proposal as if it is a marketing document, which is exactly what

it should be. In this section, write as if you are the product, not your book, because you are the item that you are trying to sell. Of course, information that you reveal about yourself must relate to your book, but the primary focus in this section must be on you. You must paint a vivid portrait of who you are and convincingly state why you're the ideal person to write this book.

Fill this section with information that will persuade a publisher to invest in you. To do so, you must understand the route your bio will travel and how your bio will be used. Then, write it in terms that will close the deal. Your biography will go to a number of different people:

- An agent and/or editor, to show him or her that you're qualified to write, promote, and make your book successful.
- The house's editorial board, to help convince it to publish your book.
- The publisher's salespeople, who will scrutinize qualifications and communicate them to booksellers to encourage them to buy your book (if booksellers show interest in your book, you usually have made the cut).

Style and Format

At best, writing about oneself can be difficult. Balancing the need to be informative without being unduly modest or excessive is often a test. Most of us are also notoriously weak at self-assessment and identifying, much less describing, our strengths can be tough.

When Writing about Yourself

If you find it impossible to write about yourself, ask some of your friends and colleagues to write a few paragraphs describing you. Request that they frame it in the context of a letter of recommendation for a job that's related to the subject of your book.

After you read their letters, make a list of the strong points they described. Usually, they will have addressed your best qualities, rather than your credentials to write the book. Expect to be surprised by how others see you; it can certainly open your eyes.

List the strong points your friends and colleagues mentioned and place them in the order that you think will most impress an editor that you're the one to write this book. Add any qualifications that your friends and associates may have omitted or may not know about, such as degrees, awards, and special activities and interests. Finally, write up your biography in narrative form and send it back to your friends for their review.

When you're working on this section:

- Write in the third person, except if your book is a personal story, and frequently refer to yourself by name. If you want to sound approachable, warm, or less formal, refer to yourself by your first name, otherwise use your last name. Choose a consistent style and stick with it throughout the proposal.
- Give only facts and information, not opinions and beliefs, unless your book is about you personally or your ideas and theories.

- Be specific. Don't say, "I've spent many years as an accountant with several large corporations." Instead write, "In my fourteen years as a Certified Public Accountant, I have worked with one of the world's largest accounting firms, Pricewaterhouse-Coopers, and for two of the world's largest corporations, General Motors and Motorola, specializing in cost accounting for equipment furnished for leased property."
- Write in a crisp, direct tone as if you were writing book jacket copy. Don't be too formal or chatty. Remember that you're writing for busy readers, so don't clog up the information you convey with unnecessary words.
- Write no more than one page; three-quarters of a page is even better.
- Be honest. Don't stretch the truth or exaggerate; it can come back to haunt you.

Start your bio with a strong lead sentence, but focus it on you, not on your book. Examine the lead sentence of the biography that Michael McLaughlin included in his proposal for *Guerrilla Marketing for Consultants*, which appears below.

Michael McLaughlin has been a partner with Deloitte Consulting, the world's fifth largest consulting firm, since 1994. In nineteen years with Deloitte Consulting, McLaughlin has sold and delivered on more than $150 million in consulting projects. He has a clear understanding of what works in the market . . . and what doesn't.

Look at this lead. What could be more powerful for a book that targets consultants? In his opening, McLaughlin immediately establishes his expert status: He is a partner with an industry leader, who has sold $150 million in consulting projects and knows the market. And notice that this opening paragraph doesn't mention the book; it's totally focused on him.

After the lead paragraph, expand on your qualifications by setting them out in the order of their relevance. If more than one item has equal importance, give, in descending order, those with the most pizzazz. Notice how McLaughlin, in his second paragraph, drives home his professional stature by stating that he worked with highly visible clients. His second paragraph reads:

> He has worked with some of America's highest-profile companies, including Sears, Procter & Gamble, Clorox, and Safeway. As Managing Partner for Deloitte Consulting Chicago, he had market responsibility for a practice of 800 consultants and served on Deloitte's Management Committee, which sets marketing strategies for Deloitte.

Since you're proposing to write a book, list your published writing credits, including assignments that you've not yet completed. Give the publisher's name and the year of publication. Mention the good reviews you received and attach copies of them at the end of the proposal. If you've written a number of published articles or reports, don't list every one, but state the number you've written and name only those that are related to the present project.

If your book is instructional, lay out your qualifications and teaching experience. Be specific. State where, when, and for whom you lectured, taught, and led workshops and seminars.

Point out your accomplishments as a speaker, advisor, consultant, and board member. State the size of your audiences if it is impressive. At the end of the proposal, provide a list of your speaking engagements and appearances for the past two years and those scheduled for the next year.

In this section, give the reader a full understanding of why you're an expert on your book's subject. Describe your hands-on experience in the field, the work you performed, the scope of projects you ran, the problems you solved, and any major players you worked with. Detail noteworthy studies or research that you created, participated in, or ran.

Platform

Since the author's platform is so critical for nonfiction, emphasize your platform in your biography. Although it's not as crucial for fiction, a strong platform can't hurt and definitely can help. So, fiction writers should touch on their major platform assets in their synopsis, without going into great detail.

For nonfiction, describe your media experience, what you've written, and where you spoke. Do you have a newsletter, and if so, how many people subscribe? Do you have a Web site? If so, how many hits does it get? Don't worry about repeating information that you included in the overview; just try to lay it out and express it differently.

Once again, let's turn to Michael McLaughlin's biography for *Guerrilla Marketing for Consultants*, which is set forth below. Note how McLaughlin highlights his media experience and names publications for which he has been interviewed as well as those to which he has contributed. He also calls attention to his public speaking experience and the fact that he publishes a newsletter that has 8,500 subscribers.

To solidify his credentials, McLaughlin states that he has an MBA, and he outlines two key association memberships: one for management consultants and the other with a speakers' association, which underlines his platform and commitment to promotion.

Finally, McLaughlin's biography provides two short sentences about him personally. The remaining portion of Michael McLaughlin's biography is reproduced below.

> McLaughlin knows how to work with the media, in print, online, television, and radio, and his opinions have been sought on the toughest business management challenges. In addition to guest appearances on local radio and television programs, he has been interviewed by publications such as *Chicago Sun-Times, Crain's Chicago Business, San Francisco Chronicle, San Jose Mercury News, Information Week,* and *Women's Wear Daily.* He has also written and published articles, including for

Computerworld, Cincinnati Business Courier, Brandweek magazine, *Chicago Sun-Times,* and *IHRIM.link.*

He has been a speaker for audiences across the country,
including Council of Logistics Management, Food Marketing Institute, Grocery Manufacturers Association, Institute
of Management Accountants, Internet World, National Millennium Panel: Business in 2005, National Retail Federation,
and Northwestern University Digital Frontiers Annual Conference. He was the keynote speaker at the Institute of Management Consultants annual conference in spring 2002.

In May 2002, McLaughlin launched Management Consulting News, a Web site and newsletter for consulting professionals. McLaughlin writes and edits the Web site content
and the monthly newsletter, *MCNews,* which grew to 8,500
subscribers in less than one year.

He is a member of the National Speakers Association
and the Institute of Management Consultants, and he holds
an MBA in Corporate Finance. He is an amateur triathlete,
and usually manages to finish races in one piece. He lives
with his wife, Sally, in Northern California.

As for providing personal information, the experts are divided.
Although it is seldom a deal maker or breaker, it does help to connect
the dots and paint a clearer picture of you.

Photographs

We live in a visually oriented world and it's getting more so. Everyone
wants pictures instantaneously; they don't want to wait or have to turn
pages.

If you look good, make the most of it. Include a flattering photograph. Editors want to see what you look like; they think that if you're
appealing, it could increase your ability to promote your book.

Have digital color photographs of yourself taken and embed the one you like best in the text of your biography section. Don't make the photograph too large, anywhere between three inches and half a page can work. Place it between paragraphs; in the beginning of the section, set off by text, or wherever you think it looks best. Test different sizes and photographs and decide what you prefer. Consider inserting more than one picture, with different poses, to see if they work, but don't go crazy.

Some commentators have noted that you have to be or look like a movie star or pass a screen test to get a book deal these days and that observation isn't too far off. Since they appeared on the TV show *The Apprentice*, some of the contestants have written published books. The publishing industry was quick to publish these mini-celebs, who also happen to look good, which illustrates how publicity driven publishing has become.

However, one agent, Liv Bloomer, states that she is "a little wary of people who enclose their photographs when she doesn't ask for them." According to Bloomer, she needs to like the content in the writer's submission before she is interested in knowing what he or she looks like.

Don't submit old photos of a younger, better-looking you. Editors will resent it and feel deceived.

Robyn Says

"When you take the photo, pretend that you're posing for your book jacket or even the book cover. Dress and pose in a manner that feels appropriate for your book and will show you as you wish to be perceived. If you want to appear distinguished, pose in business attire while seated at a desk. For your book on boating, try paddling a kayak or a canoe; take the picture for your gardening book surrounded by your prize-winning roses. If you're a speaker or in the media, include a photo of you with an audience. The goal is to communicate your platform and present yourself in a professional way."

Bulking It Up

If you don't have great credentials, take a personal inventory and list the assets you have; concentrate on everything you've done and what you do well. Don't overlook anything.

- Recall your past triumphs, everything you've accomplished and achieved.
- List the qualities that enabled you to attain those successes.
- Catalog your present skills. Are you well connected, a great interviewer or researcher, or persistent and determined?

Explore how those talents helped you come up with the idea for your book or made you the ideal person to write it. What less obvious traits of yours could be assets for selling this book?

We all wear different hats and change them to fit different occasions. Frequently, we develop a limited vision of ourselves; we pigeonhole ourselves and think that's all we are. Take a broader view; examine your talents, not just what you now do, and determine how they will be helpful to this book.

Action Steps

1. *Identify the strengths and accomplishments that make you so qualified to write this book.* Publishers want to see how you will support book sales, and not just get a list of your degrees or awards.
2. *Get testimonials that document who you are, what you've done, and where you've succeeded.* Third-party endorsements can be important.
3. *Identify an activity that you do often that reaches the most people, and focus on it.* If you frequently receive media coverage, describe all the examples that are related to the subject of your book.
4. *Describe your platform.* List what you've written, where you've spoken, and the media coverage you've received. Describe your

newsletter and how many people subscribe, your Web site and how many hits it gets.

5. *Have current photographs taken.* Submit a headshot or a photograph of you in action or before an audience. Photographs can show that you are promotable, so if you look good, capitalize on it.

Remember:

🔺 **When agents and editors receive a proposal, they wonder: "Can the author actually write this book; can he or she complete it?"** "Does the author have the qualifications to write it and will he or she deliver and energetically promote a first-rate book that will sell?" The "About the Author" section can help dispel these fears.

🔺 **In this proposal section, blow your own horn by clearly and factually showing why you're so ideally qualified to author your book.** Since your platform plays such a pivotal role in acquisition decisions, emphasize your platform in your biography. List your media experience; authorship credits; and where you have spoken, taught, and appeared. Also describe your newsletter and how many people subscribe, as well as your Web site and how many hits it gets. If you have an extensive mailing list, state its size. Providing this information will show that you can deliver the items in your promotion plan.

"Either write something worth reading or do something worth writing."
Benjamin Franklin

Promotion Plan

THIS CHAPTER WILL COVER:

► How it came about
► What publishers want
► Deal makers
► Items to include
► Sample plans

FIRST, LET'S GET CLEAR ABOUT publishers' publicity efforts. The promotional push that most writers receive is usually minimal. Unless you're a proven commodity, a bestselling author, or a big celebrity, your publisher usually won't send you on a nationwide publicity tour. If you've been dreaming about appearing on *Letterman* or *Leno*, forget about it; your odds of appearing on those shows are from zip to zero.

Publishers generally don't promote every book on their current list. Many in-house publicists promote only those titles that the head honchos designate. So publishers' publicity departments may not send news releases or review copies or try to secure interviews without express directives from above, which are not provided for all books.

Publishers' promotion budgets usually correspond to the size of the house and the amount of the advance the writer received. In most cases, larger houses spend more time, money, and effort to promote their books than smaller operations do.

If you're a "top tier" author at a house and have received a big advance, your publisher's publicity effort will generally reflect how large your advance is for that house. If you got a huge advance, expect a serious publicity push. However, even a big advance doesn't necessarily mean that the house will vigorously promote your book.

If you're an author who has not received a large advance, expect little in the way of promotion from your publisher. Sometimes, you will just get attention at the launch of your book. If your book gets a great response, your publisher will often add more resources and support. Some publishers are better than others in the publicity department. To inform yourself and avoid disappointments, talk to other authors your house has recently published. Find out if they hired their own publicists. Were they assigned a publicist, and if so, did they feel well supported?

Regardless of your publisher's efforts, roll up your sleeves and become a dedicated promoter. If you want your book to do well, you've got to promote it yourself or enlist the help of professionals. If you do it yourself, publicity is a full-time effort, and even then, most authors can't do it as well as skilled, full-time, and experienced book publicists can. You must create a plan and energetically see it through; you must move from being a writer to being a publicity machine.

Agent John Willig likes to illustrate publishers' promotional outlays by drawing a pyramid and writing "50,000 copies" along the bottom line. He then writes in "100,000 copies" in the middle of the pyramid, and "500,000" at the top. Then he states that less than 1 percent of all books published each year get into the pyramid, and only a small fraction of them ever rise to the top. Then he asks, "How much publicity do publishers provide for that less than 1 percent who sell 50,000 books or more?" And his answer is, "More than 95 percent."

How It Came About

Before you make unrealistic publicity demands on a publisher, understand the reality of the industry, how it came about, and what it means to you.

The current state of affairs is a product of the consolidation that swept through the publishing industry. As imprints merged, heads rolled. Although cuts occurred across the board, publicity departments and promotional budgets were hit hard.

This meant that fewer people had to perform more work and had fewer dollars to spend on promotion. Those who survived are slavishly overworked, so the turnover is great. If they're replaced, the newcomers are inexperienced and are paid peanuts. Therefore, they also tend to quit or sleepwalk through projects because they're so burnt out.

To fill the gap, publishers took a page from the magicians' handbook; by using sleight of hand, they pulled a rabbit out of the hat. While maintaining threadbare publicity departments, they—presto chango—magically transferred the burden of promotion from themselves to their authors. They simply decreed promotion was to be the authors' responsibility, and it became fact. Now, authors are expected to be "promotional partners," but what that really means for most writers is that the publicity burden is in their lap.

So what promotion do publishers provide? Although it varies with each house, publishers' publicists send out press releases, mailers, and review copies of your book. They will include your book in their catalogs and in trade shows, but they may not feature it. Few publishers invest in advertising for anyone other than the biggest of the big.

Publishers market and release books seasonally, in spring and fall. At the beginning of each season, publishers launch their lists of titles and have many books to promote simultaneously. It's impossible for them to give every book the same amount of attention.

Traditionally, publishers give most books a small window for success. If a book hits big, they give it more attention. If the book doesn't go so well, they move on and focus their efforts on the next book.

Publishers' promotion departments are thrilled to get just one of their authors on a national talk show at a time. If an in-house publicist books one of the house's authors on *Oprah*, it's cause for a huge celebration. However, the last thing they will do is think about why the producer didn't also book one of their other authors too.

In-house publicists will carefully orchestrate media contacts for the author with the hottest book. While their efforts are important in building relationships that might land their next big author a booking, it probably won't help you.

Being the author du jour is marvelous. Everybody loves you and wants you in their magazine or paper or on their TV show. However, few authors get swept up in such publicity frenzies! That's why authors' promotion plans and efforts are so vital to selling a book and making it successful.

What Publishers Want

Many bestselling authors are tireless and unrelenting promoters: Wayne Dyer, Deepak Chopra, Jack Canfield, Mark Victor Hansen, Dr. Nicholas Pericone, and Suze Orman, to name just a few. Selling books is a part of their business, so they work at it vigorously.

A proposal for nonfiction must include a promotion plan. For a fiction proposal, it's not necessary. But if you have some terrific ideas or connections to promote your novel, mention them briefly toward the end of your proposal's synopsis.

For many writers, writing the promotion plan is the most difficult part of a proposal. Promotion usually isn't their area of expertise. Plus, it involves the type of detailed planning and writing that they have seldom, if ever, done. However, it's really necessary. In many ways, a promotion plan is a lot like a business plan; it's a necessary exercise that forces you to think through, step-by-step, exactly what you must do to make your book a success.

To many publishers, how you tackle that task, the dedication and thought you provide, is just as important as the content that you include in your plan. They want to see the level of your effort, the organization, logic, and detail and whether they're realistic.

Since promotion plans are so important, it's tempting to promise the moon. Don't do it!

"Editors are great crap detectors," agent John Willig observes. They can sense when your promises are unrealistic. In addition, some publishers attach and make the entire book proposal a part of the contract, so you could be legally bound to deliver on your exaggerated plan.

In a promotion plan, publishers want to see that you will make a strong commitment to market your book. From your platform, they know your track record, what you've previously done. They also have a strong indication of whether you have the ability to promote your book. So in your proposal's promotion plan, they want to see the specific steps you will take. They want to see how you will build upon and expand your platform to generate sales for your book.

"The ingredient we admire most is someone is passionate about what they're doing," Kim Weiss, the director of communications for HCI Books, reveals. "Chances are that they will be useful and effective promoters. If you want to write a book and not participate in your promotion, don't expect a lot to happen. We look for people who really live and breathe what they're writing about. We have lots of experts on lots of subjects, but they're not as effective as those who really bring their hearts into what they write about."

Your promotional efforts for your book must start before the book is published and continue well after its release. Your objective should be to first create interest in your book and to sustain and build new interest.

"Nothing illustrates the importance of a writer's promotion plan better than San Francisco agent Michael Larsen's requirement for initial queries. Larsen, who wrote *How to Write a Book Proposal* (Writer's Digest Books, 3rd edition, 2004), doesn't want writers to send him query letters or even samples of their writing. All he wants is the title of their book and their promotion plan. 'Those two pieces of information alone will enable me to determine whether I can sell the book to a big house,' Larsen explains."

Deal Makers

Some writers have huge resources that they won't hesitate to pledge if it will get them book deals. As a result, they virtually agree to underwrite their books and remove much of their publisher's risk. Agent Michael Larsen calls four items "compelling" to big houses. They are:

1. *A sentence that reads, "The author will match the publisher's out-of-pocket, consumer, promotion budget up to _____ on signing."* If you're willing to put promotional money up, definitely say so. Although promotion budgets have become minuscule, most writers can't afford to kick in matching amounts. So Larsen considers this item optional. However, he believes that the following three items are mandatory.

2. *Stating the number of major markets that the author will visit as soon as the book is published.* Although publishers won't pay for your book tour, they may help you set it up and publicize it. Publicity tours are now pretty rare, unless you're a huge celebrity. Authors can offer to do them at their own cost. "Tours are time consuming and of questionable worth," according to Roger Cooper, executive vice-president at iBooks/Byron Press Visual Publications. "However, if you have an aggressive author who is highly connected with the media, tours can be extremely successful. Unless a book idea or an author is so extraordinary, first-time authors won't get publishers' support in paying for tours."

3. *Providing the number of talks the author will continue to give a year.* "If you speak, attach a list of all of your speaking engagements for the last two years and if possible, your projected engagements for the next year," Cooper advises. "This will show publishers that you have a continuity of contact with the public in your specialty area."

4. *Enumerating how many copies of the book the author will sell each year at his or her presentations.* The amount of these sales can be estimated by assuming that one of four audience members will buy the book. According to Larsen, "This is the statistic for business books, but

it seems reasonable for most kinds of books. If a quarter of your listeners hear you speak but don't want to buy your book, something is wrong, especially since you should be test-marketing your information and the salability of your talks by giving them before you try to sell a book on the subject."

It's common for authors to include a buyback commitment in their promotion plans. In at least half of the business book deals agent Edward Knappman has sold, the authors have agreed to purchase a certain number of books from the publisher at a generous discount. Usually, they sell the books at seminars, personal appearances, and through consulting practices. "To be meaningful, the buyback has to be at least a couple of thousand books," Knappman notes.

It can help for writers to state in a proposal that they will hire their own book publicist to create their publicity campaign for the book and coordinate it with the publisher. If you decide to go this route, talk first with the publicist and obtain information that you can include in your proposal's promotion plan.

Editors told us that they like when writers agree to hire their own publicist, and it can make the difference in buying books that are close calls. However, it won't be enough to rescue a book that isn't that close.

Items to Include

Specifically identify what you are willing and ready to do to promote this book. In addition to the items suggested above by Michael Larsen, list the following:

- Speaking engagements you will make.
- Seminars and workshops you will give.
- Articles you will write.
- Names of the media contacts and professional, business, and/or trade associations you will use to promote your book.

- Personal and media appearances that you will use to promote your book.
- Awards and/or media coverage you or your story have received, including upcoming events you and your story might plug into.
- Information about your publicist if you have one, highlighting if any sponsors have committed to a book tour.
- Your Web site, pointing out how many hits it gets. If you don't have a Web site, start one by immediately reserving a site name related to your book title. Name other sites and Web alliances that you are linked with as well.
- The media kit you will produce with a great press release about the book. The kit can also include a photo of the book cover, reviews and articles about the book, your contact information, your biography, the history of your career or business, a list of suggested questions, a list of your articles and appearances, brochures for your book, copies of articles on you or your subject, your photograph, endorsements, and ordering information. Other items for your kit can be an expansive article, fact sheets, questions and answers, excerpts from your book, quizzes, trivia, anecdotes, games, contests, and giveaways.
- The newsletter, online or print, for the book that will be up and running when it comes out. State how many subscribers it will reach and the alliances you have made with other well-known experts in your field to contribute to it. State how often it will be issued and the content it will provide.
- Handouts, mailers, postcards, and bookmarks with information about your book, ordering information, and the cover image.
- That you will be listed in the Yearbook Experts.
- That you will subscribe to ProfNet and PR Newswire, which reach tens of thousands of media contacts.
- Endorsements you will receive for the book.

Also see the sample promotion plans below for other items that could be included.

An Insider's Advice

Marion Gropen, who operates Gropen and Associates, a consulting firm that provides services to publishers, is a publishing insider who has the following advice for writers:

> Before authors sign book contracts, they should work with their publisher's publicity department in creative and dynamic ways. Publicity is the only type of book marketing that pays; advertising doesn't. When publishers compete for an author, they will give him or her access to their publicity departments as a sweetener to sign with them. However, they won't provide such access for authors whom they don't consider important.
>
> Try to get access and if you get it, sit down with the publicity personnel. Talk to them about what you can do when you create the book to make it easier to sell later. Get their input. Jointly develop a promotion plan where you both agree upon what you as the author will do and they as the publisher will do. Then write what you agree upon into the contract.
>
> Establish the publicity expectation up front. Publishers' publicists are tremendously overworked, but if they have an energetic, dynamic, interested, helpful, and savvy author, they will go a lot further for that author than they will for others. Remember that they are people who want to put their time and energy where it will work the best. If, from the beginning, the book has been crafted to make their job easier, it will really help. (If they're working with an author from the beginning, they may feel that they have a greater personal stake in the book's outcome.)
>
> Your plan could include hiring an outside publicity firm like PTA, which will work with the publisher's publicists to develop the book-publicity campaign. They know that they're overworked, that they have twenty times as much to do as they can possibly do in a day, so they will welcome help. If you have a plan going in on

how you're going to make this work as a team, you have a better chance of succeeding.

Include editors, designers, salespeople—everyone—from the start to make your book a "big book," even if the book wasn't originally envisioned as a big book. To get the best treatment, you want to become one of the house's big, front-list, lead titles. So start early and develop a plan where you and your publisher work as a team to create a win-win situation that will increase the profile of your book.

Unless you have a major track record, publishers may be reluctant to give you access to their publicity department before you officially sign with them. If getting particular types of promotion, such as a national book-signing tour, is vitally important to you, discuss it with your agent and agree on a strategy you can pursue. You will probably have to make trade-offs such as a lower advance or royalty percentage. Whatever you agree on regarding promotion should be included in your contract with the publisher.

After you have signed with your publisher, request a meeting with its publicity people. In order to leverage their authors' platforms, in-house publicists usually ask authors to fill out contact sheets and questionnaires listing their contacts, media relationships, and other key information. Smart authors don't just provide this information; they use it as an opening to build a close relationship with the publicist assigned to their book. Remember, in-house publicists will not just be working on your book, but they will simultaneously represent many other titles. So clearly and frequently express your appreciation for publicists' efforts on your behalf, and specifically ask what you can do to help.

Words from Willy

Willy Spizman heads the Spizman Agency (*www.spizmanagency.com*), a full-service Atlanta public relations firm specializing in author publicity.

Willy has been kind enough to give us some of his insights on book promotion, and here they are in his own words:

It's important for authors to realize that they can increase their book sales and overall success by creating a publicity partnership with their publishers. Launching publicity in today's marketplace is sometimes left to the author, not the publisher, and the window of opportunity to promote a book is narrow. Authors have the responsibility to proactively seek local and national media coverage, conduct media interviews with print and broadcast outlets, and spread the word about their book through respective circles of influence, including family, friends, coworkers, professional associations, and other colleagues. Other promotional methods include writing articles for trade publications to promote the author's expertise, securing speaking opportunities, establishing a Web site and a blog, and seeking partnership opportunities with companies. A public relations firm can assist the author in bridging all of these initiatives and broaden the reach of media opportunities.

Typically, book sales are boosted through editorial coverage and word-of-mouth vehicles created by an effective public relations campaign. Public relations differs from advertising in that it uses editorial coverage in newspapers, magazines, radio, television, and Internet sites to highlight an author and his or her book. A campaign can focus on angles and information covered in the book, developments in the news, or a great story, drama, fantasy, or any host of topics deemed press-worthy by the publicist and media representative.

Essentially, a public relations campaign works by taking information the consumer needs and wants to know and presenting it in the form of actual stories related to the book or author. The ensuing media exposure can have a huge impact on prospective book buyers. It serves to reinforce that an author is the expert on his or her subject. In addition, it lends a cachet and seal of approval that cannot be achieved by the most aggressive ad campaigns. The bottom line is that while advertising may translate into paid bias, it never occurs to the average consumer that an author might have utilized a public relations firm to secure a media spot. Not only can public relations and subsequent media exposure increase name recognition, but they can also translate into actual book sales (revenue).

The public relations firm you choose to represent you should have solid media relationships. Authors may wonder why they simply cannot write their own press releases and do the same thing as the public relations professionals. Technically, they can. However, authors must understand that the consumer media is simply not interested in press releases that are entirely self-promotional. Writing a book is much different than writing an effective press release or pitch piece. The information must be presented in a way that is palatable for laypeople, and writers and producers are indeed laypeople. Developing connections with the media is a full-time job. Public relations firms have a greater chance of solidifying connections with the press and are recognized as key sources for experts and stories.

Public relations firms initially help authors understand the marketplace by addressing a stronger position for their books and strengthening the competitive analysis specific to the books. Reviewing the marketplace reveals related titles that are already out there and then converting that information to pitch angles that will or will not work, products and experts that can help or hinder, etc. Most important, seeing this information forces the author to discover why his or her book will be different from its competition.

Another area where public relations firms can be invaluable to authors is in identifying which interviews or stories the authors should do. When authors use public relations, they must remember not to compromise themselves in the quest for media coverage. This means steering clear of media outlets that may be inappropriate because of their content or editorial slant and not compromising their beliefs to satisfy a particular editor or story. PR firms can also train authors how to conduct themselves appropriately with the media.

Once an author decides to engage the services of a public relations firm, it can often be a challenge to find the right one. Some authors who have tried PR have complained that the results were less than expected. However, this usually occurs with PR firms that have little or no expertise promoting books. Promoting books is a specialty area; it's an entirely different niche than representing fashion, entertainment, restaurants, or large corporations. In book promotion, it's of paramount importance for the publicist to speak the same language as the author and publisher. If authors have to explain publishing dates, galleys, ISBN numbers, or distribution to publicists, valuable campaign time is wasted.

As with advertising, there are no guarantees that media exposure will translate into increased book sales. A public relations firm should be able to give a prospective client some idea of what he or she can expect in terms of the media outlets to be pursued, continuity of exposure, number of weekly hours devoted to the client, as well as various strategies for a campaign. The right PR firm will have experience with related topics and some idea of how the campaign will do, and will keep detailed records of its measurable results. Public relations is a cumulative process; one television appearance or magazine article is not an adequate indicator of its merits.

Lastly, public relations is not a magical process. Those who travel this journey must be willing to be proactive participants and respond to media queries in a timely manner. Public relations, when implemented ethically and effectively, can truly establish an author as an expert and contribute to book sales.

Sample Promotion Plans

Agents usually have formats that they prefer for promotion plans. So, if you have an agent, ask if he or she can give you an example that you can review and work from.

We have provided promotion plan examples below and they differ substantially. The first is for Dr. Robert and Carolyn Turknett's proposal for *Decent People, Decent Company*. Their plan is essentially in narrative form and emphasizes the authors' extensive media credits and credentials. It outlines a few specific publicity events that they will host and fully describes the two media professionals who will jointly run the Turknetts' book-promotion campaign. The Turknetts' promotion plan is reproduced below:

Promotion of the Book

The timing for this book couldn't be better. The greed and deceit that have characterized the recent implosion of so many American corporations, and the consequent hunger from all quarters for a renewal of ethics in business, provide the perfect context for the broadest possible marketing of *Decent People, Decent Company*. Robert and Carolyn Turknett—articulate, approachable, empathic, and communicating that sureness of relationship that a husband-and-wife team is best suited to convey—are committed to pursuing every promotional opportunity for the book, and are able to do so with enthusiasm and aplomb.

The Turknetts are regular "go to" sources on issues of ethics and leadership, for numerous business writers. In recent months they have been interviewed by:

- Hal Lancaster, former *Wall Street Journal* columnist
- Chris Penttila, of *Entrepreneur*
- Erica Stephens, of the *Atlanta Business Chronicle*

- Tammy Joyner, of the *Atlanta Journal Constitution*
- Robert McGarvey, of *American Way* (American Airlines' in-flight magazine)
- Dayton Fandray, of *Continental* (Continental Airlines' in-flight magazine)
- Freelance business reporters Tom Barry, Judith Potwora, and Alan Friedman

Both Robert and Carolyn Turknett are comfortable, persuasive speakers and are often asked to address management audiences. Following the corporate scandals of 2002, they were asked to present a workshop for the Southern Institute for Business and Professional Ethics. They later presented on Leadership and Ethics to the National Association of Corporate Directors. The Turknetts are frequent panelists on topics such as employee retention, mentoring, leadership, and executive coaching at the meetings and conferences of the Society for Human Resource Management. They often address groups numbering into the hundreds from organizations such as the American Society for Training and Development, the Georgia State Human Resources Roundtable, the Georgia Psychological Association, the Sociological Practice Association, and the Organizational Change Alliance. They frequently donate their time and skills to nonprofits as pro bono contributions; in 2002, for example, they facilitated strategic planning for the Board of Directors of the Atlanta Rotary Club and led a day-long leadership-development retreat for United Way of Metropolitan Atlanta.

It's clear that the Turknetts will be effective and engaging interview subjects for both broadcast and print media.

The book will also be marketed directly by the Turknetts to past, present, and future Turknett Leadership Group clients. Prestigious past and present clients include Georgia Pacific, BellSouth, Home Depot, Deloitte Consulting, Hewlett-Packard, Kroger, Eastman Kodak, Solvay Pharmaceuticals, and the American Cancer Society. The Turknetts will leverage the contacts and clients of the Turknett Leadership Group in several ways.

- The book will be featured in TLG's newsletter, which regularly goes to 1,500 executives representing over 550 top companies.
- It will be promoted with a mailer to TLG's broader database, which contains the names of 6,000 corporate managers.

- The Turknetts will hold an open house and book signing for their considerable number of Atlanta-based clients, donate copies of the book for recognition at professional clubs they belong to, and offer to speak to professional groups that they do not belong to.
- The book will also be promoted on the Turknett Leadership Group Web sites (*www.turknett.com* and *www.leadershipcharacter.com*), which are known as high-value resources among human resource and management professionals.

In addition, the Turknetts are members of, and serve on the boards of, several organizations and frequently participate in networking events in the Atlanta area. These provide additional venues where they will promote the book.

- Carolyn Turknett is on the Advisory Board of the United Way of Metropolitan Atlanta in DeKalb County, Georgia. She currently serves on the UWMA campaign cabinet and is the Campaign Chair for DeKalb County. She also serves on the metro United Way Women's Legacy steering committee. She is active in both the American Society for Training and Development and the Society for Human Resource Management, and most recently chaired the SHRM Organization Development Professional Emphasis Group. She is also a member of the Academy of Management, the Organization Development Network, the Organization Change Alliance, and the Northlake Business Alliance.
- Robert Turknett is a member of the Rotary Club of Atlanta and currently serves on its Board of Directors. He is also a member of the American Psychological Association, the Georgia Psychological Association, the Society for Human Resource Management, and the American Management Association. He is a Georgia 100 Mentor, doing leadership development with Atlanta's top businesswomen. In the past, he has served as Leadership Chair and on the Advisory Board of United Way in DeKalb County, and has served in a leadership role on the campaign cabinet of UWMA.

The Turknetts regularly attend events such as the *Catalyst* Magazine Summits, *Business to Business* Magazine Breakfasts, the Board of Directors Network annual meeting, NACD meetings, and meetings of SHRM and ASTD. They have facilitated leadership retreats and training sessions for United Way of Metro Atlanta, the board of the Atlanta Rotary Club, the American Cancer Society, and Protestant Hour, Inc.

Decent People, Decent Company will be marketed directly to all media outlets, including television, radio, print, and the Internet. The Turknetts will be assisted in such public relations and promotion efforts by the Spizman Agency.

- The Spizman Agency (TSA) under the seasoned leadership of Willy Spizman is a full-service award-winning book promotion and media placement firm headquartered in Atlanta, Georgia. A Bulldog Award winner for excellence in national media relations and publicity, the Spizman Agency is noted for aggressive media placement and national connections. Serving as the southeastern affiliate for Planned Television Arts for twenty years, the Spizman Agency has successfully represented and worked with bestselling authors and celebrities, including H. Jackson Brown Jr., branding experts Al and Laura Ries, and the Reverend Robert Schuller. TSA also manages an innovative program for a *Fortune* 500 company, having coordinated many leading authors and personalities who have appeared at this prestigious program, including Larry King, Oliver Stone, William Diehl, The Motley Fools, Roger Ebert, Joel Siegel, Mark Victor Hansen, Trout & Ries, Stedman Graham, and Faith Popcorn. The agency has booked thousands of appearances in media outlets, including *Oprah, Today, Good Morning America, Early Today,* CNN, CNBC, CBS, MSNBC, *NBC Nightly News with Tom Brokaw, ABC Evening News with Peter Jennings, People, USA Today,* the *New York Times, Investor's Business Daily, Fast Company, Forbes, Fortune, Money, Newsweek, Time, BusinessWeek, Business 2.0, Entrepreneur, U.S. News & World Report,* the *Wall Street Journal,* and NPR. The Spizman Agency's strategic marketing campaigns have resulted in extensive book sales.

For another positive presentation alternative, consider Rick Frishman and Steven Schragis's proposal for *10 Clowns Don't Make a Circus*, which is in the timeline style. The timeline approach starts with a brief narrative introduction and then it moves into an outline format. In contrast to the Turknett plan, which concentrates on the authors' media contacts and professional credentials, Frishman and Schragis's plan itemizes in great detail what the authors will do to promote their book in terms of items and by date.

A timeline plan starts nine months prior to publication and states what the authors will do three months prior to publication, thirty days prior to publication, on publication, and ongoing, postpublication. If you decide not to use the timeline approach, consider stating at the end of your promotion plan that you will provide a timeline plan on request.

Timeline promotion plans have the advantage of putting all of your promotional efforts in a format that tells you when each item must be completed. After you create your promotion plan, you can enter the dates each item must be performed directly on your calendar.

Frishman and Schragis's plan follows below.

The authors are committed to placing their full efforts into promoting *10 Clowns Don't Make a Circus* and making the book an enormous commercial success. To do so, they will use a wide variety of promotion and publicity techniques in following the promotion plan outlined below.

PR Budget

- Purchase 1,000 copies of the book.
- Be listed in the Yearbook of Experts.
- Create the *250 Rules of Business Newsletter*.
- Establish a 250 Rules of Business Web site (*www.10ClownsDon'tMakeACircus.com* has already been secured).
- Subscribe to ProfNet and PR Newswire.

Media Campaign
- In conjunction with the publisher, create a press kit containing:
  - The book's cover art on the kit package
  - A news release on the book
  - A list of interview questions
  - A photo of the book cover
  - Photos of each author
  - Reviews and articles about the book and authors
  - Copy of the book or contact information to receive a copy
  - The authors' brochures
- Supply their lists of interested party names to the publisher.
- Send press release via the PR Newswire, which reaches over 25,000 media outlets.
- Send kits and promotional copies of the book to print, broadcast, and electronic media not on the publisher's list, using Rick's and Steven's personal media lists.
- Schedule talks and workshops on *10 Clowns Don't Make a Circus*, sell copies of the book and distribute ordering-information handouts.
- Solicit endorsements for the book.
- Implement the following promotional plan.

Speaking and Interviews
- In coordination with the publisher, Steven will arrange a five-city LEARNING ANNEX Tour at the time of publication.
- Rick will produce twenty 10-minute Morning Drive Radio Tour interviews, which his agency invented and specializes in that will run at the time of and shortly after publication.
- Rick will produce a one-hour Teleprint Press Conference with fifteen print reporters that will be run at the time of and shortly after publication.

Web Sites/Newsletters
- Develop a Web site to exclusively promote the book. The site will feature columns by the authors, articles on business rules, and submissions from readers. The site will also host contests, obtain content for future projects, and list the authors' speaking schedules.

- Create the e-mail *10 Clowns Don't Make a Circus Newsletter*. The e-mail content will be similar to that of the Web site but will concentrate more on interviews, news items, and business trends.

Nine Months Before Publication
- Write and distribute articles for business newsletters.
- Write and distribute articles for business Web sites.
- In conjunction with the publisher, design point-of-purchase graphic displays for the authors to call attention to the book at the authors' speaking engagements.
- Write articles, handouts, and ordering cards for authors to distribute at speaking engagements.
- Solicit preorders.

Six Months Before Publication
- Distribute camera-ready articles to national and major-city business, lifestyle, and women's news editors at top magazines and 200 newspapers (including *Inc., Entrepreneur,* and *Income Opportunities*).
- In conjunction with publisher, send 200 press releases to generate articles and coverage by media that focus on business (i.e., CNN Financial News, *Wall Street Journal, Fast Company, Business 2.0,* and *Wired*).
- In conjunction with the publisher, send 100 press releases to syndicated radio and TV shows that focus on business.
- Place articles and news releases in newsletters, e-zines, and Web sites such as Action Plan Marketing, Get Clients Now, Jian (developer of BizPlan Builder, Marketing Builder, Business Black Belt, etc.), American Express Business Advisory Network, MizBiz.com, Small Business Administration, Small Business Development Centers, and the U.S. and local Chambers of Commerce.
- Assist publisher in preparing flier for prepublication orders.
- In coordination with the publisher, prepare preorder postcards for distribution to national organizations such as the National Speakers Association, the National Association of Women Business Owners, Publishers' Marketing Association, and the U.S. Chamber of Commerce.

Three Months Before Publication

- Write and send press kits for the book. (Separate press kits will be customized for business groups, artists, educational institutions, and nonprofit organizations.)
- Place telephone calls daily to secure media interviews with the aim of having daily media interviews run before, at, and after publication.
- Place articles in newsletters and periodicals (e.g., *National Association of Women Business Owners, Working Woman, Bull Dog Reporter, Bottom Line*, etc.).
- In conjunction with the publisher, mail initial press-release packets with galleys, book excerpts, fliers, and reply postcards.
- Update and maintain Web sites to include current information on publicity, about the book, speaking engagements, preorders, and events.

Thirty Days Before Publication

- Forge alliances with other speakers.
- Provide excerpts from *10 Clowns Don't Make a Circus* to Web sites.
- Together with publisher, print three-fold brochures containing ten tips from the book, a copy of the book jacket, etc. Authors will mail brochures and distribute them at speaking engagements and in response to Web-site inquiries.
- E-mail first issue of *10 Clowns Don't Make a Circus Newsletter*.

Upon Publication

- Undertake a multi-city media tour.
- Give Morning Drive Radio Tour interviews.
- Send copies of the book to
  - Chambers of commerce throughout U.S. to support speaking engagements that promote the book
  - People/groups who might invite authors to present workshops
  - Members of the national media
  - Business-course professors at colleges and entrepreneurial and graduate schools
- Collect comments, personal anecdotes, and endorsements from readers.

A third and final promotion plan, the plan included in Tory Johnson and Robyn Spizman's proposal for *Women For Hire's Get Ahead Guide to Career Success* (Perigee Books, 2002) is reproduced below. This plan uses the direct narrative format to describe the authors' extensive promotional partners, media coverage, and promotional events.

Promotion Plan

This book is an absolute natural for Tory Johnson and Robyn Spizman as an ideal follow-up to the first *Women For Hire* book, which they worked tirelessly to promote. Johnson's company and career are based on connecting with thousands of diverse job seekers each year—in person at her events and online via her Web site *www.womenforhire.com.* She truly and fully understands their needs. She has developed a solid marketing strategy to attract women to her events, which she will apply to her aggressive promotion of this book.

Understanding the diverse backgrounds and interests of women, Johnson ensures that every event is marketed to a wide variety of people representing various ethnic, geographic, and educational backgrounds. *Women For Hire's Get Ahead Guide to Career Success* will become an integral component of her tireless grassroots marketing strategy.

- **Promotional Partners:** Johnson has assembled an impressive array of high-profile partners, all of which currently support and promote her career fair to their members. She will appeal to these long-established partners to embrace her second book by heavily promoting it to their members. Such partners include:

  - **National Professional Associations:** Among them are Catalyst, National Association for Female Executives, National Black MBA Association, National Association of Asian American Professionals, Financial Women's Association, Women in Technology International (WITI), Association for Women in Science, and hundreds more. Johnson will call upon these partners to promote the book through direct e-mails to their professional membership, as well as on their Web sites and newsletters. This proved very successful for the first *Women For Hire* book.
  - **On Campus:** Women For Hire partners with more than 5,000 colleges and universities nationwide, working very closely with career services offices, numerous student organizations, professors, and student alumni associations to target female candidates.

    These on-campus constituents recommend career books to their students and order them to have on hand as resources in their own offices and departments. Johnson will explore book sales to these contacts and will solicit their endorsements for the on-campus bookstores.

    In addition, as part of our partnership arrangement, the colleges send out e-mails to their students specifically recommending Women For Hire events and driving women to the company Web site. These campus e-mails reach over 1 million seniors and graduate students—all women. To promote the book Johnson will request that all e-mails include promotion for the book with a link to Amazon.com.

- **Online Recruitment:** Leading job board and recruiting sites will promote this book in direct e-mails to their registered users as part of a larger promotional agreement tied to Women For Hire events.
- **Career Fairs and Seminars:** In addition to working with diverse partners to promote this new title, the authors will sell the book at all the career fairs throughout the country. Approximately 50,000 professional women attend these events annually. Twenty events are held each year in ten major cities: Atlanta, Boston, Chicago, Dallas, Houston, Los Angeles, San Diego, New York, Tampa, and Washington, D.C.
- **Corporate Promotions:** Women For Hire has more than 1,000 clients, including *Fortune* 500 companies, nonprofit organizations, and government agencies. Johnson will solicit promotional opportunities from her clients, which would include this book as a premium incentive distributed to event attendees courtesy of a corporate sponsor. Such a book program would mesh appropriately with Women For Hire's existing corporate promotional efforts.
- **Direct E-mail:** Women For Hire has built its own proprietary database of more than 250,000 women who have requested to receive career-related information via e-mail from the company. All of these members will receive an e-mail promoting the book, with excerpts from the book and a direct link to Amazon.com.
- **Web Site:** Women For Hire's own Web site (*www.womenforhire. com*), which receives over 250,000 unique visitors each month, will feature homepage promotion of the book, including links for Amazon.com.

· **Media and Events**
- **Media Coverage:** Based on her successful organization and execution of career fairs, Johnson is recognized as an expert on issues of women's empowerment and career advancement. Each and every time she's held an event in a major market, she's received extensive local print and television coverage. Johnson

will ensure that this book becomes an essential component to those publicity efforts.

Johnson appears regularly on ABC's *Good Morning America*. In addition, Women For Hire has been featured in hundreds of local and national newspapers (including the *Wall Street Journal,* the *New York Post,* the *New York Times,* the *Boston Globe, Atlanta Journal,* and the *Miami Herald*), television programs (*Live With Regis and Kelly,* NBC's *Today Show*, CBS's *The Early Show*, CNBC's *Power Lunch*, CNN's *Business Unusual*), and Internet sites (CNN.com, Yahoo! Finance Vision, ChickClick, and Cybergrrl.com).

- **Launch Party:** Johnson's friend and talk-show host queen Kelly Ripa will host a star-studded book party in New York to celebrate the launch of the second *Women For Hire* book. In 2002 to honor the first *Women For Hire* book, Ripa hosted a cocktail party, which drew guests including Dan Rather, Paula Zahn, Deborah Roberts, George Stephanopoulos, Elizabeth Vargas, and others. Ripa and her cohost, Regis Philbin, raved about the book repeatedly on their program, which led to terrific sales. A similar effort for the newest *Women For Hire* title will be sought.
- **Seminars:** Johnson leads fee-based job-search and career-advancement seminars for more then 5,000 women each season. To promote sales of this new title, Johnson will build a book sale into the fee paid by attendees for these seminars.

Action Steps

1. *Get trained.* Media training is an excellent opportunity to prepare yourself for the media. Practice makes perfect. Check out any other speaker-training resources in your area.
2. *Make sure you have experience in radio, print, and television.* If you can't network and get yourself booked in these media arenas, hire a professional who specializes in book publicity to assist you. Even if your book doesn't end up selling, you will further position your topic and business as a result of your exposure.

3. *Prepare your talking points.* Boil down your message into three tips or points. Be in the know before you go on the air.
4. *Get creative.* Think of creative ways you can promote your book. Devise ways you will get attention, and think of yourself as an ad or a billboard for your book. Team up with an expert, a coauthor who has excellent credentials.
5. *Document everything and keep great records.* Keep a sampling of your press activities that demonstrate how marketable you will be when your book comes out!

Remember:

▲ **Publishers will look to your promotion to see how strongly you are committed to marketing your book.** From your platform, they know your track record, so they look to the promotion plan to see both the overall approach and specific steps that you will take to generate sales for your book.

▲ **Publishers want authors who are passionate about the subjects on which they write.** Authors who live and breathe and really put their hearts into their topics are the most effective promoters. Promotion plans must show that you will begin to publicize your book before it is published and will continue well after it is released. It should also show that your plan is structured to create interest in your book, to sustain that interest and to build on it.

Table of Contents and Chapter Summaries

THIS CHAPTER WILL COVER:

► Table of contents
► Advantages of summaries
► How to proceed
► Sample analysis

THE TABLE OF CONTENTS is the outline of your book. It's one of the first things prospective buyers turn to when they're thinking about buying a book. Agents and editors will do the same; they will look at the table of contents to see what information is included in your book.

A table of contents lists the subjects your book covers and shows how your book's content is organized. The chapter summaries section is an expanded version of a table of contents; it sets forth more detail on the information to be covered in each chapter. The chapter summaries section, which is also called the annotated table of contents section, gives agents and editors a deeper, more comprehensive understanding of the subject matter that your book will include and how you will handle it.

If the entire manuscript is submitted for a work of fiction, it's not necessary to include a table of contents. If you submit less than the entire book, include a table of contents so agents and editors see how the book will be developed and how it will flow.

To write your table of contents:

1. Draft a list of the chapters you plan to include in your book. First, write down all the points that you want to cover in your book. At first, just list them in the order in which they come into your mind. Don't worry about writing perfect chapter names. Start by simply listing all the content you want to include in the book. Concentrate on getting it all down on paper.

2. When you have listed all the information, reread it and then let it sit. Give it at least an hour or two or, better yet, leave it alone overnight. Then reread it with fresh eyes and a refreshed mind.

3. Return to your material and try to organize it. If given time, the mind usually puts information in logical order, and you may be surprised how quickly it falls into place. Structure the chapters as if you were telling a story. Think in terms of a beginning, middle, and end. Choose a starting point and then move sequentially from there to the end.

Don't worry about creating the perfect structure because the order of chapters frequently changes and you might decide to add

Robyn Says

"Insert a detailed table of contents for the book as a separate section immediately before your chapter summaries so it can encapsulate your book for readers in the briefest form. Although agents and editors are super speed-readers, like most busy people, they want to see a good overall picture in the shortest amount of time, and providing your book's table of contents will do the trick.

"The table of contents will give agents and editors a full overview of your book at a glance. Simply by scanning it, they will be able to see what your book is about and that your ideas are logical, well organized, and comprehensive. The table of contents will give them context and provide the foundation for the introduction and summary chapters that follow."

or delete chapters. In fact, give yourself the freedom to change and reorganize your material when it feels right. If your topics fall into at least three or four categories, consider breaking the book into sections or parts to give it a tighter structure.

4. After you decide on your list of chapters, write the titles of each chapter and section. Make the titles descriptive so that browsers can immediately understand exactly what each will cover. Write your chapter titles as if they were headlines—short, snappy, and catchy. Parody or play off popular sayings and names or the title or theme of your book. Experiment; play around with interesting combinations.

For how-to books, some experts recommend starting with numbers, such as *Ten Ways to Improve Your Posture.* They also suggest starting chapters with gerunds that end in the letters *ing*, such as *building, growing,* or *making.* For example, "Writing Lead Sentences with Punch."

Agents and editors like chapter titles that are linked to the title of your book. For example, if your book is entitled *The Managerial Cookbook: Recipes for Building Productive Teams,* start each chapter with the word *recipe* and use cooking terms such as *mix, stir, blend, a spoon full,* or *dollop.*

To create more descriptive titles, write explanatory subtitles, especially if your chapter titles are not crystal clear. But keep subtitles short, with no more than seven or eight words each. Be consistent. If you write a subtitle for one chapter or section, write a subtitle for them all.

Advantages of Summaries

Although some agents and publishers require writers to include only a table of contents in their proposals, we strongly suggest that you submit chapter summaries. Chapter summaries are advantageous because they:

- Give agents and editors more information about your book.
- Demonstrate how completely you have thought your book through.

- Provide an invaluable planning tool that helps you identify all the information you already have gathered, organize that information, and spot missing materials that you will need to write the book.
- Give you a map or blueprint from which you can write your book.

Occasionally, agents or editors may not be interested in the basic concept of a book or do not feel that it targets a sufficient audience. However, the information in chapter summaries may capture their interest, and they may suggest that you make those topics the centerpiece of your book.

How to Proceed

Writers usually hate to write the chapter summaries section because it forces them to dig deeply and to choose the precise information they will include in each chapter of their books. Writing chapter summaries is a lot of work. It takes planning, research, and plenty of thought. It requires a writer to lay out the entire book. Since so many writers learn as they write, the prospect of creating a full, well-organized outline can be intimidating.

The fears writers have about writing chapter summaries frequently stem from the fact that many mistakenly believe that once their chapter summaries are submitted in their proposals, they're cast in stone. Fortunately, the opposite is always true.

A book that is proposed or being written, and all of its constituent parts, *is always a work in progress that is subject to change.* Writing is an exploratory and learning process as much as it is an explanatory process. During that process, writers must be free to change, revise, reorganize, edit, add, and cut. Agents and editors know this and so should you!

Write full, detailed chapter summaries because they will make it much easier when you finally sit down to write your book.

To write chapter summaries, follow this general plan:

- Describe the material that will be included in each chapter. Start at the beginning of the book and work your way through. If you move from the beginning to the end, it will help your organization. It will also help you spot gaps where you need a better transition or more information.
- The amount of information you provide is up to you and your agent. Generally, include just enough to paint a clear picture of what each chapter will contain. Be consistent; don't write two six-sentence paragraphs on three of your ten chapters and only a sentence or two on the rest.
- At the least, write three to four sentences on each chapter. Usually, that's the least you can provide to demonstrate that you know the material and that it's well organized. Try not to exceed five- or six-sentence paragraphs for a chapter. If you find that you have too many topics, reorganize or consolidate some points. Don't ramble, try to fill, or fudge.
- If possible, begin some chapter descriptions with an anecdote, story, or quotation that foreshadows the content that will come. Then explain what the chapter will cover, the questions it will answer, or the problem it will solve.
- If you plan to provide a foreword or a preface, follow the same procedure.
- If others are going to write introductory material, identify them by writing a one-sentence biography. Add another sentence on the gist of what they will write.
- If you plan to include back matter such as appendixes, forms, a glossary, or recommendations lists, identify them after your chapter summaries. After you list all back matter, describe only those items that are special, unique, and will add value to your book.

Bullet points can be good alternatives to narrative chapter summaries. Instead of spelling out what will be included in each chapter, just bullet the main information and ideas. Bullets can be terrific for proposals for books that are loaded with advice or tips because they outline the meat in each chapter without overwhelming readers.

Sample Analysis

In his proposal for *Big Cotton: How a Humble Fiber Created Fortunes, Wrecked Civilizations, and Put America on the Map* (Viking Books, 2004), Stephen H. Yafa walked readers through the logical progression of information that he would provide in each chapter of his fascinating book.

Yafa, a veteran journalist and award-winning screenwriter, confesses that, "Writing the table of contents section was the hardest part; I really labored over it. But it was also the most productive because it forced me to really lay out the book and decide exactly what it would include. It was definitely worth all the work I put in."

Excerpts from Yafa's proposal appear below:

---

5. CAMELOT ON THE MERRIMACK

How cotton initiated the industrial revolution, first in the United Kingdom through Arkwright and then in America at Lowell, Massachusetts, whose textile mills were built from machine designs stolen from England. How Lowell became America's industrial showplace, employing single women who left home for the first time in history to find work in its mills. How Northern mills' magnates, the Lords of the Loom, aligned themselves with their suppliers, the Lords of the Lash, wealthy Southern planters, until conscience and cotton finally clashed.

6. SOUTHERN EXPOSURE

How and why the South left itself open to a civil war it could not win, based on its erroneous belief that England would come to its aid because

---

of the U.K.'s reliance on raw Southern cotton. How the South's dangerously outmoded European feudal structure was fixed in time from the moment Eli Whitney, an unemployed 27-year-old Yankee teacher, invented his seed-separating gin in 1793. How the South's cotton monoculture also doomed it to rely on a free labor force—slavery—and westward expansion: two factors that brought it directly into conflict with the federal government. Firsthand plantation owner and slave narratives re-create the mood and conditions of the times.

7. BOLL WEEVIL BLUES

Why cotton is such an arbitrary despot. Just as the crop seemed to revitalize the South in the decades following the Civil War, creating jobs when New England's textile mills moved across the Mason-Dixon line, cotton's enfant terrible appeared. How a tiny bug that crossed into Texas from Mexico in 1892 and migrated east wiped out most of the country's cotton crop. A look at the massive devastation it left behind. How the pesticides used to combat the weevil, derived from WWI nerve gas, created a dependence on toxins in growing cotton that has increased over time.

Action Steps

1. List three examples of how chapter summaries can be helpful.
2. Post a sign where you write saying that a book is always a work in progress.
3. Write a list of the chapters you plan to include in your book. Don't worry about their titles. Just concentrate on listing what each will be about.
4. Link chapter titles to the title of your book. Reinforce your book's title and content through your chapter names.
5. Think of anecdotes, stories, or quotations that you can include at the beginning of each chapter summary.

Remember:

 The table of contents section of a proposal tells agents and editors what information is included in the book and how the book is organized. It gives them a thumbnail sketch of what the book is about and how clearly and logically it's constructed.

 A chapter summaries section is an expanded version of a table of contents that provides greater detail on the information that will be covered in each chapter. The chapter summaries section is also called the annotated table of contents section, and it gives agents and editors a deeper, more comprehensive understanding of the book's subject matter and how it will be handled.

Sample Chapters

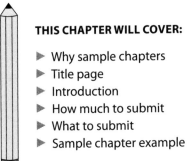

THIS CHAPTER WILL COVER:

▶ Why sample chapters
▶ Title page
▶ Introduction
▶ How much to submit
▶ What to submit
▶ Sample chapter example

BEFORE THEY BUY, publishers want to sample the merchandise; they want a taste of how your book will read. Can you blame them? You are asking them to invest in you, so it's understandable that they want to be sure that you write well and have something to say.

For most unpublished authors, it's impossible to sell a manuscript without submitting sample chapters. Celebrities and publishers' girl-friends are the rare exceptions. First-time fiction writers are usually asked to submit the whole book so editors can determine if it holds together. Even many established writers are asked to send sample chapters.

Sample chapters can be your demo, your showcase, the giveaway, or example that clinches your book sale. By the time agents and editors read your sample chapters, they will know a lot about you and your book. They will know that you have a great idea and the type of cre-dentials, platform, and focus they want. Now, they want assurances that you also write well, which your sample chapters can provide.

Sample chapters give publishers a strong indication of writers' organizational and writing skills. How a writer builds a chapter provides insight into how he or she will develop the book. Most nonfiction books have to flow logically, and editors usually won't buy those that don't.

The Value of Sample Chapters

Writers often resent being required to submit sample chapters. It can force them to do lots of work, and it doesn't guarantee that their proposal will sell. Often, they respond by subconsciously giving less than their best effort. Frequently, their submissions turn out to be halfhearted, and some of their resentment seeps through.

If you feel such resentment, carefully review whatever you plan to submit. Then, have your sample chapters read by your most trusted critics, and instruct them to be ruthlessly truthful with you. Editors pay

Robyn Says

"In my book proposals, I like to include the title page of the proposal after the chapter summaries and immediately before samples of my writing begin. I simply include the same title page that is page 1 of the proposal.

"As we said, the title page should identify this document as a proposal for a book. It should also state the title of the book and the subtitle and give the author's name. Some people also include contact information, which doesn't have to be repeated, especially if it's given in the header that we suggested that you include.

"Including the title page again signals agents and editors that a sample of the content that will be in the book is about to begin. Essentially, including the title page again is a decorative device, but it also introduces the writing that will be included in the book and it changes the proposal's tone and mood."

close attention to sample chapters and too much could be riding on your submission for you to unknowingly sabotage your own work.

Sample chapters can have additional and far-reaching benefits. It's not uncommon when agents and editors reject submissions for them to comment on how well writers write; some even offer advice. In an industry filled with "no thank yous," encouragement or tips can be just the nudge you need to keep you going.

Sample chapters can also prove to be door openers because agents and editors who see something in your samples may invite you to contact them again regarding future projects. While this connection may be slim, it is a connection in a world in which such connections are elusive. You may be able to leverage that connection to get your future submissions read.

When you have such an opening, start your subsequent submissions to the agent or editor by referring to his or her comments, advice, or invitation to contact him or her again. For example, "Thank you for your great advice regarding my query letter last year and for inviting me to contact you again."

Introduction

Unlike most experts on book proposals, we recommend that you include the introduction to your book in your proposal. Include it immediately after your chapter summaries and before the sample chapters.

The introduction to your book gives agents and editors a window into the soul of the book. They can get a fuller sense of what your book is about, why you want to write it and what you hope it will achieve. The introduction is an ideal spot for you to show your passion, belief, and commitment to your subject and to lay out your approach.

The introduction can be a great vehicle to capture an agent's or editor's attention and make him or her want to read more. However, don't just submit your introduction as your only chapter; always include it with one or more sample chapters.

How Much to Submit

When it comes to sample chapters, submitting two solid chapters is usually enough, but more than most writers want to send. Publishers will accept one sample chapter if your idea is great and you've been published before. How much you should submit varies from house to house and project to project, so send in two sample chapters to be safe. For submissions to publishers, rely on your agent's advice. Agents know the market and the best ways to proceed.

"Agents and publishers are making investment decisions, so the more information you can provide to convince them that their investment will be a wise one, the better your chances of making a deal," agent John Willig observes. "One thing to do is send them more of the manuscript and make sure that it's very well written. It's becoming more like fiction, in which you submit the complete manuscript, which eliminates the risk that the writer won't deliver what was promised. Although the accepted wisdom is that you only need to submit a chapter or two, it may be wise to submit more, even the completed manuscript."

What to Submit

Submit a representative sample, writing that fully shows your writing style, format, organization, and approach. If your book is broken down into a list, such as *100 Ways to Make Money in Real Estate* or *Veggies from Artichokes to Zucchini*, submit at least six or seven good samples to show agents and editors what each chapter will contain. Take the same approach with books of your art, photographs, or illustrations.

To select the samples to submit, review the chapter summaries in your proposals. The best candidates should be clear; they should jump right out at you. If you've prepared the summaries correctly, they will provide a blueprint for the chapter you will write.

The sample chapters you submit should show both your command of the subject and your writing talent. So look for chapters in

"If you have more chapters written, consider submitting them because they could make publishers feel more comfortable about you and your book. If you can send the entire manuscript, better yet, because it will show the publisher exactly what they're buying.

"Include your estimate of the number of pages each chapter will run alongside each chapter name. Although your numbers will be estimates, they will help editors get an idea of your book's length. The size of the book you will be expected to deliver may be set forth in your publishing contract, so don't inflate your estimated page counts."

which you can display both. If the revelations in one of your chapters are groundbreaking or sensational, send that chapter. Make your submission so gripping that editors will crave more.

Only submit sample chapters that have been thoroughly edited, reviewed, and polished. Since these chapters are going to represent you, submit nothing but your best. Use these chapters to show how clearly and readably you write.

Author Don'ts for Sample Chapters

Writers often want to submit their first chapters; frequently they're already written or the content is fresh in their minds. The danger in submitting early chapters is that they often repeat information previously stressed in your query, proposal, or introduction. Also, they may not include material that is the strongest or the most fascinating part of your book.

Don't send chapters with repetitive or weak material. Besides being skilled readers, agents and editors are also incredibly busy. When they finish reading your sample chapters, they have lots more to read. So when they come across repetitive or weak information, they may not give your sample their full attention or may think that you made less than an acceptable effort to provide something new, fresh, or strong.

Also avoid submitting chapters that simply introduce or summarize material that you plan to discuss in greater detail subsequently in your book. They usually don't provide a good sampling of your writing.

Submit chapters that show you, your concept, and your writing in the best light. Also try to submit examples that will reflect the rest of the book.

Sample Chapter Example

For *10 Clowns Don't Make a Circus*, Rick and Steven Schragis proposed a book that would consist of 250 separate vignettes about business dealings. So they submitted a number of samples to show the publisher precisely what they proposed to provide. One of those chapters appears below:

The Value of Face-to-Face Meetings

E-mail, intranets, faxes, voice mail. They're fine for accelerating the transfer of factual information. But when your communication involves any emotion at all—such as the expressing of different opinions—a face-to-face meeting is by far the best bet, with a traditional, interactive phone conversation a distant second choice.

Why is face-to-face communication so important? As we get more efficient at communicating facts electronically, we tend to forget how much emotion we convey through body language and voice tone. For example, as I say with words that I disagree with someone, my tone, my posture, my smile, and my eye contact may at the very same time be saying, "I value and respect your opinion and enjoy working with you . . . even though I disagree with you on this point."

Meeting people individually can help create or cement the bonds of a good working relationship. There's something that's just more

---

down-to-earth, genuine, and satisfying about communicating in person. On a group level, participative meetings give people a feeling that their opinion can be heard, and that it counts!

Action Steps

1. View your sample chapters as opportunities to show agents, editors, and then the world your great idea and how well you write.
2. Determine if providing more sample chapters will be worth the time and effort involved.
3. Reread your sample chapters with an eye toward their organization. Is all content presented clearly and logically?
4. Review your chapter summaries to decide which chapters to write and submit as samples.
5. Check that the samples you submit show you in your best light and make your material sound fresh.

Remember:

⚠️ **Sample chapters give publishers concrete examples of your organizational and writing skills.** From sample chapters, publishers can get strong indications about the caliber of the writing you can produce. Most nonfiction has to flow logically, and editors usually won't buy those manuscripts that don't.

⚠️ **Most publishers want authors to submit two sample chapters with their proposal, but the submission requirements vary from house to house.** If you have more chapters written, consider submitting them because receiving more material could give the publishers higher levels of confidence about you and your book. It is better yet if the entire manuscript can be sent, because it will show the publisher exactly what it is buying.

CHAPTER 16

Frosting on the Cake

THIS CHAPTER WILL COVER:

▶ Endorsements
▶ Spin-offs
▶ Appendixes and attachments
▶ Press materials
▶ Resources needed

TO THIS POINT, THE INFORMATION that we've provided to you in this book sets forth the basic items that you should include in your book proposal. However, a number of additional items can also be submitted, depending on you and the type of book you are proposing.

In preparing book proposals, creativity helps. Agents and editors respond to new and different ideas and approaches. They see so many queries and proposals that the unusual can catch their eye.

Think boldly and creatively. Test your approaches on your friends, colleagues, and advisors before you submit them. If they tell you that they are too outlandish, too cute, or in bad taste, you can always scale back.

During your research, see the approaches similar books take. Then ask what you could do to improve upon that. For example, if they have an interesting feature, could you adapt it and utilize it somewhere else that would give your book more impact? Constantly see how you could do it differently and better.

Endorsements

Enlisting the support of well-known and/or well-respected individuals can help book sales. Such individuals can help in many ways, by writing your book's foreword, preface, or introduction. Or they can provide an endorsement for your book that can be placed on the book's cover, back cover, first few pages, and/or promotional materials.

Endorsements usually help when they're from individuals that most people recognize or who have a large following. The head of your local chamber of commerce, a city supervisor, or another local bigwig may love your book and have lots of clout close to home, but if your writing doesn't target your local area, their endorsements may not carry much weight with agents and editors.

On the other hand, Robyn feels, "It's very important and smart to get endorsements from real people like the readers who are right beside you in the trenches, not just the success stories. People identify with real people, who may have gone through the same problems that they now face. I've mixed in the names of unknowns for years because what they say is important."

Frequently, authors unrealistically think that celebrities will love and endorse their books—if only they can reach them. Editors frequently see proposals that state that the authors will approach the biggest names for endorsements for their books. Be realistic. Celebrities are inundated with endorsement requests and may not respond to yours. Even if you have a great contact, think twice before mentioning it in your proposal, because so many "close contacts" never pan out. When you have a reliable contact to a celebrity, describe your contact in the proposal or, better yet, get the endorsement and include it in the proposal.

Spin-offs

The traditionally accepted wisdom is that publishers prefer to work with authors who can produce families of books rather than those who will write only one or two titles. However, this may no longer be universally true. While publishers still love authors who can write a series of books, which can turn into annuities for publishers, most now judge each book on its individual merit, and then they think about the future.

Acquisitions, first and foremost, are based on the book proposed, not future promise. However, showing thought, research, creativity, and an understanding of the market in a proposal can be influential. These factors won't rescue a weak or flawed proposal, but they may be a factor that helps to tip the balance in favor of an author.

Developing ideas for spin-offs can be fun-filled and creative. It can allow you to brainstorm and explore other expressions of your subject or approach. Some of these ideas might work well as part of the book you propose or even strengthen it so that it's more attractive to agents and editors. Unfortunately, most writers feel that they're expected to submit a laundry list of spin-off titles, and in doing so, they get carried away. After proposing a few logical, interesting future titles, they drift far afield and propose preposterous books.

Appendixes and Attachments

Writers and agents append various materials to the end of proposals. Many include press packages to stress the authors' platforms, clippings, lists of speaking engagements, articles they've written, and even tapes of their appearances.

Writers also include food, candy, and all sorts of gifts. Even if you're writing a pastry cookbook, think twice before you send your chocolate chip cookies. Although some agents and editors will love them, others will be turned off. Unless you come up with something truly new and amazing, they won't sway most agents and editors because all they really care about is the book.

If you speak regularly, attach a list of your speaking engagements for the past two years. Also include a list of the engagements that you have booked for the coming year.

If you have written articles or a regular column, include copies of them. If you or your subject has received recent media coverage, include copies of the stories of listings when features have been aired.

"Samples of features can be included as an attachment at the end of the proposal or in an appendix," according to book packager Leanne Chearney. "But be careful that they don't appear too fragmented, out of context or look just like a jumble of things attached at the end because somebody is less likely to read them and understand how they work. If there are elements that repeat, you can include them at the end in a discrete appendix."

Press Materials

Since promotion plays such a major role in selling books, many writers collect articles and press clippings when they've been covered in the media. Then they submit them with their book proposals.

Agents and editors want writers who are media savvy. They also want to see that authors have both experience and a strong track record with the media, because it indicates to them that the writers can successfully promote their books. Press clippings can convincingly show them a writer's strong history with the media.

Resources Needed

Authors often need additional substantial resources to complete their books. Frequently, they have to incur expenses to get permissions to use copyrighted materials and for travel, research, artwork, and other features.

Although these expenses are usually borne by the author, many writers identify them in proposals in order to justify larger advances. Some even itemize the projected expenses they expect to pay. Identifying and itemizing expenses also demonstrates that the author has fully appraised the task at hand.

Which, if any, of these expenses publishers will pay, and how they will pay them, differs with publishing houses and with the nature of the book proposed. For example, those who publish lifestyle books may pay for travel, photography, and design. Agents usually know publishers' practices and who will underwrite what.

Publishers tend to be more amenable to paying expenses involved in obtaining permissions or those needed to reproduce art, design, and photography in books. They may build these expenses into the royalty offers they tender to writers or provide them in separate advances or grants. Unlike advances, grants are outright payments that don't have to be earned or paid back. They're not commonly given, but it may not hurt you to ask.

"When media-savvy authors appear on radio or TV, they ask producers to send them e-mails confirming that they were outstanding guests. Usually the producers are happy to comply, especially if the guests were great. The writers keep these endorsements and then package them with the press materials that they include with their book proposals. A bunch of enthusiastic endorsements thanking a writer for his or her fabulous media performances can be a major plus."

Action Steps

1. Focus on the spin-offs that make sense. Do not include every gadget, gizmo, and talk show that could occur because of your book, but rather only the best ideas.

2. Don't water down your book by showing how many book ideas you have. Focus on the big one, but mention the supporting cast if they are really outstanding.

3. Show proof that the market has interest in your spin-offs. Perhaps you could include a letter from a producer or stores who would be interested in your product line if the book gets published.

4. If you have a great platform, include press packages with clippings, lists of speaking engagements, articles you've written, and even tapes of your appearances.

5. Identify the resources you will need to complete your book, such as funds for permissions to use copyrighted materials and for travel, research, artwork, and other features. Then request them from the publisher.

Remember:

⚠ **Including endorsements in your proposal praising you or your book can impress publishers because endorsements can boost book sales.** It may also help to include your ideas for spin-offs of your book because publishers like to develop series of books and establish brands. Although good spin-off ideas may help, acquisition decisions are based primarily on the book proposed, not on future promise.

⚠ **If you speak regularly, list your speaking engagements for the past two years in an appendix** to your proposal as well as your bookings for appearances during the coming year. Include in the appendix copies of articles or columns you have written and articles or information about media coverage you have received.

chapter 17

What Agents and Publishers Hate

THIS CHAPTER WILL COVER:

▪ The top twenty things that agents and publishers hate

WRITERS WHO WANT TO GET their books published must learn new rules and protocols in order to make the best impression on agents and editors. Unfortunately, many don't. Often, writers find these rules counterintuitive because they're contrary to the way they usually operate. Unfortunately, their mistakes can alienate agents and editors and be fatal to their book's chances of ever reaching bookstore shelves.

When we conducted interviews to gather information for this book, we specifically asked agents and editors to tell us their pet peeves. Our purpose was to compile a list of no-noes that could guide authors on what they should avoid. Although we've already discussed much of what our interview subjects pointed out, we believe that this information is so important, it is worth reiterating it here.

The following are twenty things that agents and editors hate.

#1: *Writers claim no competition exists*

Competitive or comparable books usually exist. Rarely does a book have no competition. Yet authors regularly claim that nothing like their book has ever been published.

When agents and editors hear this claim, they wince. Except in rare cases, it means that the writers haven't done their homework. Unless they understand their market and exactly which books will be their competition, they won't know where their book fits into the market. As a result, it will usually be less focused and unique.

#2: *Writers claim their books will be the next blockbuster*

Although it's essential for authors to be enthusiastic about their books, it's equally important that they be realistic. Excessive expectations can make it difficult for writers to get agents or editors and can send book projects off course.

Agents and editors have options. They know that unrealistic writers usually won't take their advice and can be difficult to work with. Many have keen sensors and won't subject themselves to working with difficult authors, whom they're probably going to disappoint. They tell us it's just not worth the aggravation.

#3: *Writers say how much others liked their books*

Agents and editors simply don't care what others think about a book unless they are (a) book-publishing professionals or (b) celebrities or published authors who are willing to endorse the book. Even then, their opinions don't carry much weight and will rarely influence the agent's or editor's decision.

A large part of being a literary agent or an editor revolves around taste and editorial and business intuition. Most have a keen sense about books and take great pride in their understanding of the market as well as their ability to recognize what makes a successful book. Frequently, these instincts have been honed by years of experience, and agents and editors rely heavily on them. So, don't waste time telling them that your reading club loved your book about the life of some obscure rock 'n' roller. It won't get you anywhere; in fact, it will probably turn them off!

#4: *Submissions are made for books on subjects that the agent or editor doesn't handle*

Sending submissions that recipients don't handle wastes everyone's time, yours and theirs. So don't send your memoir to an agency when the guidebooks and agency Web site clearly state that it doesn't represent memoirs. Agents' and editors' time is precious, and sending such submissions can alienate them. Information on the types of books that agents and publishers handle is easily found in guidebooks and online. Writers can also call and ask what type of books agents, publishing houses, and specific editors handle.

Sending correspondence to an agency on topics that it doesn't handle indicates to agents and editors that the writer is lazy and hasn't done his or her basic homework. And if the writer hasn't gotten the basics down, agents and editors reason, he or she probably won't be able to accomplish what it takes to write a successful book.

#5: *Correspondence is not addressed to a particular agent or editor*

Don't address any correspondence, especially submissions, generally or to "Dear Agent or Editor." It's impersonal and it makes your communiqué look like a form letter that you simply dashed off to a slew of agents or editors.

How much notice do you pay to mail you receive that is not addressed to you but is sent to "Resident"? Why should agents and editors react differently? They want to feel that writers specially selected them to handle their book; that authors conducted research and contacted them because they found certain qualities that could make a good fit.

One more thing about addressing correspondence: Don't send mass e-mails that reveal the names of all those you e-mailed. How would you react if you received a request asking you to consider entering into a rather personal business relationship, which was also sent to fifty of your competitors?

Agents and editors informed us that they constantly receive e-mail submissions that are also addressed to a ton of other agents and editors. While most don't mind writers sending submissions to others, the fact that writers are so sloppy really turns them off. Be more professional. Learn how to send multiple e-mails that each disclose only the name of the recipient who receives it.

#6: Writers make undocumented assertions

When some authors contact agents and editors, they simply state that their work is good and expect that alone will be sufficient to convince the recipient to request them to submit a proposal or manuscript. Agents and editors need more information. Save everyone time and energy by describing the work in order to let agents and editors decide if they might be interested in it.

Send a one-page query letter or e-mail to create further interest in your work. Agents and editors are busy and don't have time to play guessing games or e-mail tag with writers who are unwilling or unable to tell them about their proposed books.

#7: Writers call constantly, are demanding, and don't let up

It makes no sense to put undue pressure on agents and editors. Remember they're in the business of getting books published—so let them do their jobs. The demands and pressures on them are enormous. Don't increase their burdens, because it could backfire on you.

Be reasonable, patient, and understanding. Agents and editors know how important your book is to you, but their hands may be tied. Publishing is built on relationships, and you can't create strong, long-lasting, mutually beneficial relationships if you excessively pressure publishing professionals.

#8: Writers try to be cute, instead of being direct and straightforward

In children, cuteness can be adorable. In adults, it seldom works; in fact, it usually becomes irritating. Agents and editors don't have time for cuteness. They want to know, in a few words, what your book is about, and why you're the perfect person to write it. They're much less interested in how cute and clever you are.

Sprinkling cute and clever material in your work can be effective if it's not overused and is creative. The problem is that writers get hooked on their cuteness, mesmerized by their own cleverness, and think that's how they must write. Before long, they're concentrating so hard on being cute and clever that they shortchange the content and quality of their words.

#9: *Writers send submissions in strange formats and colors*

Some writers love, or need, to attract attention. Frequently, they can't sense when they cross the line and draw the wrong kind of attention.

Attract interest in your writing by providing top-quality work. Great ideas expressed in clear, well-crafted sentences that are built with the most vivid words will speak more convincingly than outlandish colors and designs. Gain attention through your ideas and prose and don't diminish them by being flashy and inappropriate.

#10: *Writers have a bad attitude or act superior*

Acting as if you're entitled to an editor's attention will instantly turn him or her off. As we said before, writers can be myopic. Some are totally filled with themselves and their work or are captivated by the perception of their own brilliance. Usually, their vision is skewed, and worse yet, they treat agents and editors rudely and disdainfully.

Get a reality check. If you are truly brilliant, treating others poorly will tarnish your glow and increase the difficulties of getting published. It takes little to be pleasant and considerate. Give it a try. Let the quality of your work speak for itself, especially if your attitude tends to drive others away. You know who you are!

#11: *Writers demand unrealistically high advances*

Some writers, including those who are unpublished, insist on guarantees that they will receive hefty sums for their books. Usually, they have no reasonable basis for their demands and suffer from a highly inflated view of their worth.

Although it's important that authors be paid fairly, even well, harness your expectations. It takes time to become an established writer and get what you think you're worth. Unrealistic demands can sabotage your writing career or, at least, impede it, and agents and editors may be unavailable when you call. If you consistently produce good work and energetically promote it, you'll eventually get what you're worth.

#12: *Publishing bigwigs kill a deal*

Editors and everyone on a publisher's editorial board loves a book, but the rep at Barnes & Noble isn't sure about it, which damns the book to oblivion. Sometimes people just don't get it; they miss the special essence of a great book and, sadly, a fine book dies.

The power of giant booksellers can make or break a book deal. Publishers often check with them before they buy books. A rep's veto is fatal. If the rep isn't enthusiastic or is even just lukewarm, the publisher will probably pass.

#13: *Writers reject professional advice*

Some writers won't listen to constructive criticism from their agents and/or editors. They're not open to reworking a proposal to make it better. Trust the people who are publishing your book and don't think that you know more than they do about the publishing process. Some authors end up sabotaging their books because they think they know more than their agents and editors.

Smart authors are willing to listen. Although agents aren't infallible, they are professionals; selling books is their business and they bring a perspective to book projects that authors usually lack. Smart authors listen and are open to ideas that can enhance their books.

#14: *Writers are unprepared*

Some writers never bother to learn how to write a query letter and a proposal, which are authors' main marketing tools. They simply throw together a bunch of information and think that their books will be sold because of the genius of their ideas. Usually, their submissions have no structure.

Agents and editors want to work with professional writers who have taken the time to learn precisely what they should submit and how it should be submitted. Writers who don't do their homework are generally work and aggravation intensive down the line, which busy publishing professionals don't need.

#15: Writers are unrevealing

Some writers don't disclose anything about their background and credentials. Those who do not have strong credentials may deliberately omit them out of fear of seeming inadequate, while others with excellent credentials may be overly modest.

To sell you and your book, your agent or editor needs to know who you are and what you've done to convince others in the acquisition chain of the value of buying your book.

#16: Writers constantly tinker

Don't burn out your agent or editor by constantly tinkering with your material and constantly resubmitting new or revised versions. He or she could get frustrated and scrap you and your many versions.

Work on your submission until you feel satisfied, then stop and leave it alone. Don't make additions, deletions, changes, or revisions unless they're specifically requested. Take your best shot and then let your agent or editor try to sell it.

#17: Writers claim bogus referral sources

Frequently, agents and editors told us that writers contact them and say they were recommended by a person the agent or editor never heard of. Usually, it's either a scam or the writer botched the name of the referral source.

If someone takes the trouble to recommend you to his or her agent or editor, make the effort to get that individual's name right. When you contact agents and editors, the point is to impress them, not to come off like some scatterbrained ditz.

#18: *Writers don't include a sample chapter*

Many writers don't want to submit a sample chapter; they want to sell their book idea and then go and write the book. Publishers need to see writing samples. Most feel that writers know that they should submit a sample chapter or two, and when they don't, it makes the publisher feel that the writer is lazy or deceptive.

#19: *Authors say, "I will match the publisher's marketing contribution up to X number of dollars"*

If you're going to spend money, then simply state that you'll spend money and precisely how much. Saying you'll match what the publisher spends is vague and infers that, "I'll only do it if you do it."

#20: *Authors state they will approach celebrities or authorities for endorsements or interviews when they have no way of reaching them*

If writers state, "I will pitch Oprah Winfrey with this project," they should explain in the proposal their connection to her. Otherwise, editors might question other promises made in the proposal.

CHAPTER

18

Summing Up

NOW THAT YOU have read this book, we wish you good luck on your journey toward becoming a published author. We hope that you have a long and fulfilling writing career. Remember during your journey that you are the only person on earth who can make your dreams of becoming an author come true. Your destiny is in your hands.

Congratulations for reading this book, for taking the first step by becoming informed about the process and the business you hope to enter. Unfortunately, not everyone who reads our words will get a book deal. What separates those who get published from the pack is the quality of their book ideas and their willingness not to give up.

Persistence and perseverance are vital. Breaking into publishing is difficult and demanding. Many try, but most don't succeed. It requires you to continually give of yourself and make changes. Often, those changes are painful and discouraging, but they're essential for you to learn and grow.

Writing is a process of trial and error, of learning from your mistakes and making the necessary corrections to reach your goal. It takes time and constant effort, thinking, shaping, editing, rewording, rephrasing, reorganizing, and rethinking until you get it right.

Keep at it, stay with it, and don't give up. Burnish your writing skills, refine your ideas, learn about the market, and find your niche.

Spend time with other writers; talk about the craft, the business, and what you must do. Keep working and follow the suggestions we've made, and we hope to see you on the shelf.

Get Started

Now, it's time to go to work if you haven't done so already. Find a subject that fuels your passion, something that excites, intrigues, and motivates you. Passion enlarges your ideas, gives them power and color. Passion makes your words more descriptive and alive. When you write with passion, the pages fly because you have so much to say.

When you're writing with passion, you can feel it physically. The words form in your mind as fluid sentences. The ideas jump out in logical and powerful sequence. Your body tingles and your mind feels light. You feel elated and excited. It's a rush.

We can't teach you passion; it's something you must find yourself. It's there, but you must find the trigger . . . and then pull it, let it go.

When it comes to writing, an element of passion that's often overlooked is passion for success: that fire to not just write well, but to write excellently. This passion is what enables writers to endure constant topic changes, rewriting an idea or even scrapping it and beginning another.

To become an author, you must clearly see your book, understand your role, live it, breathe it, and never give up, no matter what. And when we say no matter what, we really mean it! The best ideas often die before they have time to develop. And then they are published by someone else, and you can hear yourself saying, "I thought of that idea years ago!"

We can't stress the following point enough: Rejection must be your fuel, and the word *no* your motivating force. Closed doors must encourage you to simply work harder to figure out how to break through the barriers of the publishing world. Sadly, the timid and those individuals who give up easily won't survive *Author 101*.

With that said, it is our genuine hope that you, too, will have your book published, that your dream of becoming an author will become your reality. Obviously, we can't promise you that outcome, but if you work hard, dedicate yourself to writing the best book ever, fully prepare, be totally relentless, and network like crazy, you just might be one of the lucky writers to actually reach that goal.

So, good luck on your journey! And along the way, please feel free to contact us about this book or to send your comments and questions to *www.author101.com*.

Glossary of Publishing Terms

PUBLISHING INDUSTRY PERSONNEL tend to speak in shorthand that they assume everyone understands, which is not always the case. When they talk about books and publishing, they can completely lose you. For example, publishing people constantly refer to "trade books," which can leave industry outsiders scratching their heads.

Unless you ask for clarification, important information about your proposal or book deal can sail completely over your head. Familiarize yourself with the following lingo so when you chat with agents and publishing personnel, you can understand what they're saying and be sure that you're both on the same page.

ABA

See American Booksellers Association.

acquisitions editor

An editor at a publishing company who has the responsibility to obtain and screen manuscripts that the house may wish to publish.

advance

This term is used in two ways, to mean

(1) An advance against royalties, which is the amount that a publishing company pays an author on signing a book contract and prior to publication, and

(2) The number of copies of a book ordered from the publisher prior to the book's publication.

advance copies

The version of a book that is sent to reviewers and booksellers prior to publication. They are usually not the final version, may have a different cover, and may not be fully corrected.

agent

See literary agent.

ALA

See American Library Association.

American Booksellers Association (ABA)

The major industry association for U.S. booksellers. Its annual trade show, BookExpo, is where people in the industry display and learn about new publications and products.

American Library Association (ALA)

The oldest and largest library association in the world. Has members in academic, public, school, government, and special libraries.

Association of American Publishers (AAP)

The industry association for large book publishers.

auction

The process in which publishers bid to obtain the rights for books.

backlist

Titles that publishers released prior to the current season and are continuing to sell.

backmatter

Material provided in a book after the text. Can include appendixes, glossaries, recommended books, and resource lists.

blurbs (cover copy)

Short quotes from successful authors, reviewers, or publications in praise of an author or book. Usually placed on the front and back covers and first few pages to promote the book.

boilerplate
Standard contractual clauses or language. Generally, they are subject to negotiation and change.

book clubs
Groups that sell and send designated books to their members at regular intervals and at reduced prices.

BookExpo America (BookExpo)
The mammoth annual trade show sponsored by the American Booksellers Association that is attended by thousands of publishing companies and publishing-related businesses.

book proposal
See proposal.

Books in Print
An R. R. Bowker publication that lists books currently in print. Generally available in library reference departments.

bulk sales
Books sold in volume to a single purchaser at a discounted price.

coagent
An agent who works with a writer's agent usually on specialized

subsidiary rights such as film, foreign language translations, and television rights. Also known as subagent.

copyediting
Review of manuscripts for errors in spelling, grammar, punctuation, syntax, and meaning. Copyediting is a part of the publishing process that is done by professional editors at the publisher's expense.

copyright
The federally protected property rights granted to creators that control how a book and other works may be used by others.

co-op ads (cooperative advertising)
Advertisements run by booksellers that are partially paid by publishers to promote their books.

cover copy
See blurbs.

cover letter
A transmittal letter or e-mail sent to an agent, editor, or publisher with a book proposal, manuscript, or other material.

critique fees
See evaluation fees.

dust jacket
See jacket.

earned out

An author has earned out when he or she has earned royalties in an amount that equals the advance against royalties that the publisher previously paid him or her.

evaluation fees

The charges made by agents to read and critique writers' book proposals, manuscripts, or other materials.

first serialization

The publication of selected portions of a book in periodicals prior to the book's publication. *See also* serialization and second serialization.

flap copy

Text on the inside portion of a book cover that usually describes the book.

foreign rights

The rights that authors give publishers to enter into contracts to publish their books in other languages and sell them abroad.

galleys

A prepublication version of a book. Galleys, which are also known as galley proofs, are typically sent to the author for review and final correction before the final version is produced.

genre

The general classification of a book such as business, parenting, writing, etc. The genre is usually indicated at the top of the back cover.

hardcover

Books bound in a stiff, protective cover that usually resists bending.

imprint

A publishing company that is a division or subsidiary of a parent company. For example, Pocket Books is an imprint of Simon & Schuster, Inc.

ISBN

The International Standard Book Number (ISBN) is a ten-digit number that identifies each title and publisher. It's used for ordering and inventory purposes.

jacket

The removable covering placed on most hardbound books that contains promotional material on the book. Also called the dust jacket.

juvenile

The term often used for children's books.

lead sentence/paragraph

The first sentence or paragraph in a piece of writing.

list

Books that a publisher has published that are still in print. A list can include books from the publisher's current season and its previous seasons.

literary agent

The representative who sells the author's work to a publisher. An agent usually negotiates the book contract and receives a percentage of the income generated by the book.

LMP

Literary Market Place (R. R. Bowker). A directory of the publishing industry that is published annually.

mail order

Sales of books by publishers directly to buyers that do not go through booksellers or other intermediaries.

manuscript

The complete version of a book that is submitted for publication.

mass market

Books sold at retail outlets other than traditional booksellers. Includes warehouse stores, department stores, newsstands, and specialty stores. For example, a store that specializes in selling games may sell a book on chess.

midlist

A book that doesn't make the best-seller list. The term is also used for authors of midlist books.

option

The right that authors grant their publishers giving them the first opportunity to acquire their next book.

out-of-print (OP)

Books that a publisher no longer prints or has in stock.

overview

The opening section of a book proposal that describes the book and its market. Also called the introduction, summary, synopsis, or vision.

packagers

Those who bring the concepts for book projects to publishers and then supervise the creation of the products that the publishers release. They frequently work with writers, designers, and others to bring their projects together.

platform

An author's following and media presence. Usually means that the author has achieved renown as a frequent speaker and/or writer, for hosting a popular Web site, for having a large list of names, or for receiving wide media coverage.

premium

Books sold in volume at a discounted price as part of a promotion.

primary rights

The basic rights that a publisher acquires from an author when it acquires the author's books. *See also* subsidiary rights.

print on demand (POD)

A process that prints only books that have been ordered. POD books can be printed one at a time as opposed to in large print runs.

proofreading

Editing of manuscripts and galleys to correct any spelling and grammar mistakes, catch typographical and typesetting errors, and review appearance of pages. This is usually done after the copyediting stage, and is performed by professional editors at the publisher's expense.

proposal

The format in which publishers require books to be submitted in order for them to consider the books for publication.

publication date

The date when a book is delivered to retailers for sale. Also referred to as the "Pub date."

Publishers Weekly (PW)

The main publication providing information to the publishing industry.

query or query letter

A written submission to agents and editors to determine if they would be interested in representing an author, publishing an author's book, or learning more about the book. Queries via e-mail have recently become more popular.

remaindered

Books that are offered for sale well below their cover prices. Usually they are books that didn't sell well or that have been around for a while.

reprint rights

The authorization to republish a book, or to publish different versions or formats of it, after its initial publication.

reserve

Funds that are not paid out to authors in order to meet a stated contingency. In publishing, amounts in reserve are held for books that the publisher estimates will be returned by booksellers.

returns
Books that haven't sold and are returned to the publisher. It's standard practice in the book-publishing industry to allow retailers and wholesalers to return books that haven't sold.

review copies
Free copies of a book that are sent, usually prior to publication, to book reviewers and other media people.

royalties
The amount that authors receive from publishers for the sales of books and subsidiary rights. Royalties are usually calculated as a percentage of the income generated by the book.

SASE
The abbreviation for "self-addressed, stamped envelope," which should be included with authors' submissions to agents and publishers if they want their submissions returned.

secondary rights
See subsidiary rights.

second serialization
The publication of selected portions of a book, usually in

periodicals, after the book has been released. *See also* first serialization *and* serialization.

self-published
The term for a book that an author publishes him- or herself and not through a traditional publishing company. Typically, the authors handle all writing, editing, design, printing, and distribution themselves. *See also* vanity publishing.

serialization
The publication of selected portions of a book in periodicals. *See also* first serialization *and* second serialization.

sidebar
Additional information included in a manuscript's text that is usually placed in a box or a shaded area or set off in another design format.

slush pile
The place where unsolicited manuscripts are placed before they are read by editors.

special sales
Book sales made to outlets other than traditional booksellers. Frequently, these sales are for a large number of books.

subagent
See coagent.

subsidiary rights

The rights to reprint, serialize, and reproduce a book for movies, television, audio and video recordings, and electronically.

textbooks

Books created for and sold to educational markets.

trade books

Books sold through traditional channels to bookstores and book clubs.

translation rights

The authority to publish a book in languages other than the language in which it was originally published.

unagented

An author or a book that is not represented by a literary agent.

unsolicited

A submission that was not requested by the recipient. Usually refers to queries, proposals, or manuscripts sent to agents, editors, and publishers.

vanity publishing

The process in which an author pays a company to publish his or her manuscript. Some vanity publishers also provide editing, design, and distribution services.

Resource Directory

IN CREATING THIS DIRECTORY, we have tried to include the best resources and the most up-to-date information about them. However, resources continually change: They move, merge, refocus the direction of their business, and even shut down. In addition, when you refer to this list, it may be long after we compiled it, so some information may not be current. To be on the safe side, check the resource directory on our Web site, *www.author101.com*, which should have the latest information.

> **LEGAL NOTICE:** This list is provided strictly as a resource guide and to inform you of the resources that may be available to you. Readers should independently check all information about these resources before using them. The authors and publisher specifically assume no liability for the use of this resource directory, nor do they guarantee its accuracy.

BOOK PUBLISHING

R. R. Bowker, 630 Central Avenue, New Providence, NJ 07974; Tel: (888) 269-5372. E-mail: *info@bowker.com*.
www.bowker.com

BookMarketing.com. John Kremer's online warehouse of information on book publishing, marketing, and promotion.
www.bookmarket.com

Information Today, Inc., Literary Market Place **(LMP),** 143 Old Marlton Pike, Medford, NJ 08055-8750; Tel: (800) 300-9868; Fax: (609)

654-4309. E-mail: *custserv@infotoday.com*. This directory of the publishing industry includes lists of publicists, publishers, agents, lecture agents, organizations, media, writers' conferences, trade services, and international resources.

✍ *www.literarymarketplace.com*

Para Publishing. Dan Poynter's site provides tons of information on publishing. Free documents and statistics plus books, reports, disks, and tapes.

✍ *www.parapublishing.com*

Publishers Marketplace. Electronic newsletter that tracks deals, sales, reviews, agents, editors, news. Includes Publishers Lunch Deluxe.

✍ *www.publishersmarketplace.com*

Publishers Weekly. The news magazine of the book industry that is read by most major publishers. Reports on all segments of the industry, including creation, production, marketing, and sales.

✍ *www.publishersweekly.com*

The Book Standard. Reports on the book market by giving sales figures, analyses, news, reviews, commentary, job boards, and database resources.

✍ *www.thebookstandard.com*

BOOK PROMOTION

PMA: Independent Book Publishers Association, 627 Aviation Way, Manhattan Beach, CA 90266; Tel: (310) 372-2732; Fax: (310) 374-3342. E-mail: *info@pma-online.org*. Runs the PMA Publishing University, which is usually held the two days before the annual BEA trade show begins.

✍ *www.pma-online.org*

BestSeller Mentoring, Randy Gilbert and Peggy McColl, 398 E. Eaglewood Lane, Mt. Jackson, VA 22842; Tel: (540) 856-3318. E-mail: *support@bestsellermentoring.com*. *Make Your Book an Online Best Seller.* Learn how to sell tons of books online and get onto the bestseller list for Amazon.com, Barnes & Noble, Books-a-Million, 800-CEO-READ, etc.

✎ *www.BestSellerMentoring.com*

PR Leads, Daniel Janal, P.O. Box 130, Excelsior, MN 55331; Tel: (952) 380-1554. E-mail: *dan@prleads.com*.

✎ *www.prleads.com*

PUBLICITY SERVICES

Planned TV Arts, Contact: Rick Frishman, 1110 Second Avenue, New York, NY 10022; Tel: (212) 593-5845; Fax: (212) 715-1667. E-mail: *Frishmanr@plannedtvarts.com*. PTA is one of the leading book publicity firms in the United States, specializing in radio, print, and national TV and radio placements for all authors. They work with major publishers (Random House, Simon & Schuster, Rodale, etc.) and love small publishers, too!

✎ *www.plannedtvarts.com*

Rick Frishman. You can get Rick's Million Dollar Rolodex at *www.rickfrishman.com*.

The Spizman Agency, Contact: Willy Spizman, Atlanta, GA; Tel: (770) 953-2040. E-mail: *willy@spizmanagency.com*. The Spizman Agency is a full-service public relations firm that specializes in marketing, promoting, and publicizing books, products, and leading-edge experts. They have worked with many bestselling authors and publishers as well as with first-time authors launching their books and literary careers. The Spizman Agency oversees the Think About It program at Turner Broadcasting and serves as the Atlanta affiliate of Planned Television Arts. The agency focuses on print and broadcast placement, book development, and comprehensive book consultation.

✎ *www.spizmanagency.com*

AceCo Publishers, Alex Carroll, 924 Chapel Street #D, Santa Barbara, CA 93101; Tel: (805) 962-7834; Fax: (805) 564-6868. E-mail: *Alex@RadioPublicity.com.* Web: *www.1shoppingcart.com/app/aftrack.asp?afid= 29117. Alex Carroll's Radio Publicity Home Study Course.* The ultimate in learning how to get yourself booked on the largest radio shows.

✍ *www.RadioPublicity.com*

North American Precis Syndicate, Jim Wicht, Empire State Building, 350 Fifth Avenue, 65th Floor, New York, NY 10118; Tel: (212) 309-0139; Fax: (800) 990-4329. E-mail: *jimw@napsnet.com.* NAPS National Newspaper Feature Service. Covers 10,000 newspapers nationwide. A great way to get feature stories on your product or book published in daily and weekly newspapers throughout the country . . . at very low cost. Tell Jim that Rick Frishman sent you, to get a special bonus.

✍ *www.napsnet.com*

Metro Editorial Services, 519 Eighth Avenue, New York, NY 10018; Tel: (800) 223-1600; Tel: (212) 223-1600. E-mail: *mes@metro-email.com.* Prepares and sends a feature news story to more than 7,000 newspapers monthly. Also sends out themed material to targeted audiences.

✍ *www.metroeditorialservices.com*

PR Newswire, 810 Seventh Avenue, 35th Floor, New York, NY 10019; Tel: (212) 596-1500; Tel: (800) 832-5522. Sends news releases to targeted or all media nationally and internationally.

✍ *www.prnewswire.com*

Bradley Communications, 135 E. Plumstead Avenue, P.O. Box 1206, Lansdowne, PA 19050-8206; Tel: (610) 259-1070; Tel: (800) 784-4359; Fax: (610) 284-3704. *Radio TV Interview Report.* Sends a description of your expertise and media pitch to more than 4,000 media outlets.

✍ *www.rtir.com; www.freepublicity.com*

Pneuma Books, LLC. 327 Curtis Avenue, Suite Five, Elkton, MD 21921; Tel: (410) 996-8900; Fax: (410) 996-8901. The premier book development, design, and marketing solution for publishers; not a subsidy publisher or vanity press.

✍ *www.pneumabooks.com*

Foster Covers, George Foster, Book cover designer, 104 S. Second Street, Fairfield, IA 52556; Tel: (641) 472-3953; Tel: (800) 472-3953; Fax: (641) 472-3146. E-mail: *foster@lisco.com*.

✍ *www.fostercovers.com*

RJ Communications, Ron Pramschufer, 51 East Forty-second Street #1202, New York, NY 10017; Tel: (800) 621-2556; Fax: (212) 681-8002. E-mail: *Ron@RJC-LLC.com*. Has thirty-plus years in the business, specializing in all areas of the design and manufacture of fiction, nonfiction, and children's picture books. Free e-mail and telephone consultation.

✍ *www.BooksJustBooks.com*

Penelope Paine, 817 Vincente Way, Santa Barbara, CA 93105; Tel: (805) 569-2398. E-mail: *PPPennyP@aol.com*. Specializes in children's books and selling to school systems.

Jane Centofante, 10616 Rochester Avenue, Los Angeles, CA 90024; Tel: (310) 475-9758; Fax: (310) 474-0814. E-mail: *jfcento@aol.com*. Editor of nonfiction bestsellers; edits manuscript for content and structure so it's publisher-ready.

Media + (Media Plus), Judith Kessler, 828 Westbourne Drive, West Hollywood, CA 90069; Tel: (310) 360-6393; Fax: (310) 360-0093. E-mail: *jude001@earthlink.net*. Award-winning writer/creative consultant in all forms of media, including book proposals and media training.

Quinn's Word for Word, Robin Quinn, 10573 West Pico Boulevard #345, Los Angeles, CA 90064; Tel: (310) 838-7098; Fax: (same). E-mail: *quinnrobin@aol.com*. Copyediting, writing, proofreading, manuscript evaluation, and ghostwriting. We make your ideas sparkle.

Cypress House, Cynthia Frank, 155 Cypress Street #123, Fort Bragg, CA 95437-5401; Tel: (707) 964-9520; Fax: (707) 964-7531. E-mail: *qedpress@mcn.org*. Editing, production, and promotion services for new publishers. Personalized and reasonable.

GHOSTWRITERS

Mark Steisel, Tel: (415) 454-9161, (415) 454-0125. E-mail: *msteisel@earthlink.net*. Rick's favorite ghostwriter.

Tim Vandehey. E-mail: *tim@pacificwhim.com*.

Word Wizard, David Kohn, 3117 Lake Shore Drive, Deerfield Beach, FL 33442; Tel: (954) 429-9373. E-mail: *WordWiz@gate.net*. Award-winning ghostwriting, editing, manuscript analysis, coaching. Twenty-five years of experience.

Mahesh Grossman, Tel: (561) 434-9044. E-mail: *getpublished@authorsteam.com*.

COPYRIGHT AND PUBLISHING ATTORNEYS

Lloyd Jassin, Esq., The Actors' Equity Building, 1560 Broadway #400, New York, NY 10036; Tel: (212) 354-4442; Fax: (212) 840-1124. E-mail: *Jassin@copylaw.com*.
✎ *www.copylaw.com*

Charles A. Kent, Esq., 1428 de la Vina, Santa Barbara, CA 93101. Tel: (805) 965-4561.

Law Offices of Jonathan Kirsch, 1880 Century Park East, Suite 515, Los Angeles, CA 90067; Tel: (310) 785-1200. E-mail: *jk@jonathan kirsch.com.*

Ivan Hoffman, Attorney at Law, P.O. Box 18591, Encino, CA 91416-8591; Tel: (818) 342-1762; Fax: (419) 831-2810. E-mail: *ivan@ivan hoffman.com.*

✐*www.ivanhoffman.com*

Venable, Jeff Knowles, 1201 New York Avenue NW #1000, Washington, DC 20005; Tel: (202) 926-4860. E-mail: *jdknowles@venable.com.*

✐*www.venable.com*

Joel Berman Esq., 780 Third Avenue, New York, NY 10017; Tel: (212) 583-0005. E-mail: *joel@joelsberman.com.* Every type of legal issue. Wills, estates, and if you need to sue someone.

CLIPPING SERVICES

Bacon's Clipping Bureau, 332 S. Michigan Avenue #900, Chicago, IL 60604; Tel: (312) 922-2400; Tel: (800) 621-0561; Fax: (312) 922-3127.

✐*www.bacons.com.*

BurrelleLuce Press Clipping Service, 75 E. Northfield Road, Livingston, NJ 07039; Tel: (973) 992-6600; Tel: (800) 631-1160; Fax: (973) 992-7675.

✐*www.burrellesluce.com*

BurrellesLuce Press Clippings, 589 Eighth Avenue, 16th Floor, New York, NY 10018; Tel: (212) 279-4270; Fax: (212) 279-4275.

Canadian Press Clipping Services, 2206 Eglinton Avenue E. #190, Toronto, Ontario M1L 4T5, Canada; Tel: (416) 750-2220, ext. 203.

Newsclip Clipping Bureau, 363 W. Erie Street, Chicago, IL 60610; Tel: (800) 544-8433; Fax: (312) 751-7306. E-mail: *clip363@aol.com.* ✍*www.newsclip.com*

Freebies, 1135 Eugenia Place, P.O. Box 5025, Carpenteria, CA 93014-5025;Tel: (805) 566-1225; Fax: (805) 566-0305. E-mail: *freebies@aol.com* or *freebies@earthlink.net.* Linda Cook, editor. Published five times a year with a circulation of 350,000 paid subscribers.

ONLINE BOOKSTORES

Amazon.com—*www.amazon.com*

Barnes & Noble—*www.barnesandnoble.com*

Borders—*www.borders.com* (now teamed with Amazon.com)

BOOK WHOLESALERS

Baker & Taylor—*www.btol.com*

Ingram Book Group—*www.ingrambook.com*

MEDIA DIRECTORIES

Information Today, Inc., 143 Old Marlton Pike, Medford, NJ 08055-8750;Tel: (609) 654-6266; Fax: (609) 654-4309. E-mail: *custserv@infotoday. com. Literary MarketPlace* (*LMP*) has lists of book reviewers and talk shows as well as publicists. The first place to check out media directories is at your library. See what they offer and how much they cost, and then decide how to get what you need.
✍*www.literarymarketplace.com*

Bacon's Information, 332 S. Michigan Avenue #900, Chicago, IL 60604; Tel: (800) 621-0561. *Bacon's Media Calendar Directory* lists the lead editorial calendars of 200 daily papers and 1,100 magazines. Important if your book's sales are keyed to a holiday. Includes a free bimonthly newsletter.
✍*www.bacons.com*

R. R. Bowker, 630 Central Avenue, New Providence, NJ 07974; Tel: (888) 269-5372; Fax: (908) 771-7704. E-mail: *info@bowker.com*. Publishes *Broadcasting & Cable Yearbook* and *Ulrich's Periodicals Directory*.
✐ *www.bowker.com*

BurrellesLuce, 75 E. Northfield Road, Livingston, NJ 07039; Tel: (973) 992-6600; Tel: (800) 631-1160; Fax: (973) 992-7675.
✐ *www.burrellesluce.com*

Adweek Directories, 1515 Broadway, New York, NY 10036.
✐ *www.adweek.com*

The Yellow Book Leadership Directories. Leadership Directories, 104 Fifth Avenue, New York, NY 10011; Tel: (212) 627-4140. Directories of media, associations, law firms. The Web site has media and industry news.
✐ *www.leadershipdirectories.com*

AceCo Publishers, Alex Carroll, 924 Chapel Street #D, Santa Barbara, CA 93101; Tel: (805) 962-7834; Fax: (805) 564-6868. E-mail: *Alex@RadioPublicity.com*. *Alex Carroll's Radio Publicity Home Study Course*. Offers a database of radio stations as well as a course on getting publicity via radio phone interviews.
✐ *www.1shoppingcart.com/app/aftrack.asp?afid=29117*

Media Distribution Services, 307 West Thirty-sixth Street, New York, NY 10018-6496; Tel: (212) 279-4800; Tel: (800) 637-3282. Has lists for all media. Will blast-fax, print, and mail.
✐ *www.mdsconnect.com*

Infocom Group, 5900 Hollis Street #L, Emeryville, CA 94608; Tel: (510) 596-9300; Tel: (800) 959-1059. E-mail: *info@infocomgroup.com*. *National PR Pitch Book* and *Bulldog Reporter's MediaBase* custom lists.
✐ *www.infocomgroup.com*

"The Tip Sheet"—Monthly newsletter by Planned TV Arts, 1110 Second Ave., New York, NY 10022; Tel: (212) 593-5820. To sign up, go to *www.plannedtvarts.com*.

Open Horizons, P.O. Box 205, Fairfield, IA 52556; Tel: (641) 472-6130; Tel: (800) 796-6130; Fax: (641) 472-1560. E-mail: *info@book market.com. Book Marketing Update.* A twice-monthly newsletter about promotion. Editor-in-Chief John Kremer, author of *1001 Ways to Market Your Books.* Provides marketing tips and techniques, Internet sources, and media contacts.

✆ *www.bookmarket.com*

Infocom Group, 5900 Hollis Street #L, Emeryville, CA 94608-2008; Tel: (800) 959-1059. E-mail: *Bulldog@infocomgroup.com. Bulldog Reporter.*

✆ *www.bulldogreporter.com*

Partyline, 35 Sutton Place, New York, NY 10022; Tel: (212) 755-3487. E-mail: *byarmon@ix.netcom.com.* New media, interview opportunities.

✆ *www.partylinepublishing.com*

Speaker Net News, 1440 Newport Avenue, San Jose, CA 95125-3329; Tel: (408) 998-7977; Fax: (408) 998-1742. E-mail: *editor@speakernetnews. com.* A free weekly newsletter aimed at speakers. Also provides valuable ideas for writers.

✆ *www.speakernetnews.com*

Ragan Communications, 316 N. Michigan Avenue, Chicago, IL 60601; Tel: (800) 878-5331. *Ragan's Media Relations Report.* Provides information on trends, media tips, and interviews.

✆ *www.ragan.com*

CONFERENCE RESOURCES

How to Build a Speaking and Writing Empire, a seminar run by author Mark Victor Hansen (of the *Chicken Soup for the Soul* series). For a brochure, call (800) 423-2314.

Literary Market Place and the May issues of *Writer's Digest* and *The Writer* magazines list writers' conferences.

ShawGuides—*www.shawguides.com/writing*

Maui Writer's Conference—*www.MauiWriters.com*

WEB SITE DESIGN AND MANAGEMENT

Rick's Cheap Domains. Get domains for $8.95.
✑*www.rickscheapdomains.com*

Membership101. Create your own membership Web site.
✑*www.membership101.com*

Web Solutions. Solutions for managing your Web sales and marketing.
✑*www.rickswebsolution.com*

PlanetLink, P.O. Box 5428, Novato, CA 94948; Tel: (415) 884-2022. E-mail: *sales@planetlink.com*. Works with businesses that want an Internet game plan and a Web site that works. Web site design services, search engine promotion, hosting and Internet consulting.
✑*www.planetlink.com*

Phil Huff, P.O. Box 14, Mt. Pleasant, SC 29465; Tel: (843) 568-5640. E-mail: philhuff@philhuff.com.
✑*www.themarketingwebmaster.com*

Artslynx International Writing Resources. Lists organizations for writers and has links to other sites.
✍ *www.artslynx.org/writing*

Associated Writing Programs. Includes lists of college writing programs and writers' conferences.
✍ *www.awpwriter.org*

Book Flash. Provides links to news releases and other publishing information.
✍ *www.bookflash.com*

Book Talk is an archive of articles about publishing and links.
✍ *www.booktalk.com*

BookWire. Click on *Publishers Weekly* for a free subscription to a daily dose of publishing news. The site also provides links to other helpful sites, including dozens of online marketing companies.
✍ *www.bookwire.com*

Chip Rowe's Book of Zines. Provides info about zines and a network of zine editors.
✍ *www.zinebook.com*

Cluelass. A network of mystery writers.
✍ *www.cluelass.com*

CSPAN. For information on the cable TV station's book programming, go to *www.booknotes.org*.

FeatureSource, Bruce Lansky, 5451 Smetana Drive, Minnetonka, MN 55353; Tel: (800) 338-2232, ext. 112. E-mail: *blansky@featuresource.com*. A free content source for print, broadcast, and electronic media.
✍ *www.featuresource.com*

Frugal Fun. Shel Horowitz, the author of *Marketing Without Mega-bucks*, offers free monthly Frugal Marketing Tips and other helpful information.

✐ *www.frugalfun.com*

Gebbie Directory. Mark Gebbie provides links and e-mail addresses that will enable you to V-mail (send video e-mail to) the media. Gebbie Press specializes in online promotion.

✐ *www.gebbieinc.com*

HTML Writers Guild hosts a network of Web authors and offers help on writing and marketing for the Web.

✐ *www.hwg.org*

The Northern California Independent Booksellers Association. Offers a free newsletter by Pat Holt, a former *San Francisco Chronicle* book review editor and publishing's I. F. Stone.

✐ *www.nciba.com*

The Onion. Provides humor breaks and, by example, wisdom about writing humor.

✐ *www.theonion.com*

Pilot Search. Lists 11,000 writing links.

✐ *www.pilot-search.com*

ProfNet. Provides a link to authors and other experts for journalists and 11,000 public relations professionals.

✐ *www.profnet.com*

Put It in Writing. Jeff Rubin puts twenty-five years of journalism experience into making newsletters as effective as possible.

✐ *www.put-it-in-writing.com*

Ralan Conley's SpecFic and Humor Webstravaganza. Has information on humor and sci-fi markets, and 600 writing links.
✑ *www.ralan.com*

ShawGuides. Provides information on writers' conferences and workshops.
✑ *www.shawguides.com/writing*

Speaker Net News. A free weekly newsletter aimed at speakers that also provides valuable ideas for writers.
✑ *www.speakernetnews.com*

Visual Horizons. Designs for "200 On-Screen/MS Word," along with help on using them.
✑ *www.visualhorizons.com*

Writer's Digest. Includes daily publishing news, information about promotion, and writers' conferences.
✑ *www.writersdigest.com*

The Writer's Toolbox has resources for novelists and journalists.
✑ *www.writers-toolbox.com*

WORKSHOPS

Besides workshops, the following organizations provide a wealth of information, online and offline, about publishing and promotion.

The Jenkins Group, Jerrold Jenkins, 400 W. Front St., Traverse City, MI 49684; Tel: (231) 933-0445; Tel: (800) 706-4636; E-mail: *jenkinsgroup @bookpublishing.com.*
✑ *www.bookpublishing.com*

Open Horizons, John Kremer, P.O. Box 205, Fairfield, IA 52556; Tel: (641) 472-6130; Tel: (800) 796-6130; Fax: (641) 472-1560. E-mail:

info@bookmarket.com. John is the author of *1001 Ways to Market Your Book*. He also edits the *Book Marketing Update* listed above and conducts three-day Book Marketing Blast-Off Seminars.

✍ *www.bookmarket.com*

Para Publishing, Dan Poynter, P.O. Box 8206-146, Santa Barbara, CA 93118-8206; Tel: (805) 968-7277; Tel: (800) PARAPUB; Fax: (805) 968-1379. E-mail: *info@parapublishing.com*.

✍ *www.parapublishing.com*

PMA: Independent Book Publishers Association, Jan and Terry Nathan, 627 Aviation Way, Manhattan Beach, CA 90266; Tel: (310) 372-2732; Fax: (310) 374-3342. E-mail: *pmaonline@aol.com*.

✍ *www.pmaonline.org*

Small Publishers Association of North America (SPAN), P.O. Box 1306, Buena Vista, CO 81211.

✍ *www.spannet.org*

BestSeller Management Consulting, Greg Godek, 5641 La Jolla Hermosa Avenue, La Jolla, CA 92037; Tel: (858) 456-7177; Fax: (858) 456-7155. Works with two clients per year in getting them on the bestseller lists.

Cross River Publishing Consultants, Thomas Woll, 3 Holly Hill Lane, Katonah, NY 10536; Tel: (914) 232-6708; Tel: (877) 268-6708; Fax: (914) 232-6393. E-mail: *twoll@pubconsultants.com*. Author of *Publishing Profit*. Consults on general management issues, publishing economics, editorial analysis, etc.

✍ *www.pubconsultants.com*

"BACK OF THE ROOM" BOOK SALES

Fred Gleeck. Tel: (800) FGLEECK.

✍ *www.fredgleeck.com; www.theproductguru.com; www.selfpublishingsuccess.com; www.infoproductsseminar.com*

239

Media and Back of the Room Sales Training. Joel Roberts, media trainer extraordinaire. Tel: (310) 286-0631.

VIDEO MEDIA TRAINING

Book Marketing Works, 50 Lovely Street, Avon, CT 06001; Tel: (860) 675-1344; Tel: (800) 562-4357. E-mail: *info@strongbooks.com*. *You're on the Air*, a must-have video created by Brian Jud, in which producers for major shows discuss how to prepare for and give interviews. Comes with two companion books by Jud: *It's Show Time: How to Perform on Television & Radio* and *Perpetual Promotion: How to Contact Producers and Create Media Appearances for Book Promotion*. He offers other videocassettes and audiocassettes.

✐ *www.bookmarketingworks.com*

WRITERS' ORGANIZATIONS

For the most part, the following are national organizations. *Literary Market Place* lists many others that are statewide or regional.

The Academy of American Poets, 588 Broadway, Suite 604, New York, NY 10012; Tel: (212) 274-0343; Fax: (212) 274-9427. E-mail: *academy@dti.net*.
✐ *www.poets.org*

American Medical Writers Association, 40 W. Gude Dr., Rockville, MD 20850-1192; Tel: (301) 294-5303, Fax: (301) 294-9006.

American Society of Journalists & Authors (ASJA), 1501 Broadway, Suite 302, New York, NY 10036; Tel: (212) 997-0947; Fax: (212) 768-7414. E-mail: *asja@compuserve.com*. Has chapters around the country and an annual conference.

The Authors Guild, 31 East Twenty-eighth Street, 10th Floor, New York, NY 10016; Tel: (212) 563-5904; Fax: (212) 564-8363. E-mail:

staff@authorsguild.org. Provides a wide range of services and publishes a newsletter for its 7,200 members.

✎ *www.authorsguild.org*

California Writers, 2214 Derby Street, Berkeley, CA 94705. Is dedicated to educating writers of all levels in crafting and marketing their writing. Has chapters throughout California.

✎ *www.calwriters.org*

Christian Writers Guild, P.O. Box 88196, Black Forest, CO 80908; Tel: (866) 495-5177 (toll free); Fax: (719) 495-5181. E-mail: *nvrohrer@spiralcomm.net*. Offers a study course and workshops.

✎ *www.christianwritersguild.com*

Dog Writers' Association of America (DWAA), 173 Union Road, Coatesville, PA 19320; Tel: (610) 384-2436; Fax: (610) 384-2471. E-mail: *dwaa@dwaa.org*. Sponsors annual competitions and monthly newsletter for writing about dogs and dog competitions.

✎ *www.dwaa.org*

Editorial Freelancers Association (EFA), 71 West Twenty-third Street, Suite 1504, New York, NY 10010; Tel: (866) 929-5400 (toll free); Fax: (212) 929-5439. A nonprofit, professional organization for self-employed workers in publishing and communications.

✎ *www.the-efa.org*

Education Writers Association, 2122 P Street, NW, Suite 201, Washington, DC 20037; Tel: (202) 452-9830. E-mail: *ewa@crosslink.net*. A professional association of education reporters and writers.

✎ *www.ewa.org*

Freelance Editorial Association, P.O. Box 38035, Cambridge, MA 02238-0835; Tel: (617) 576-8797. E-mail: *freelanc@tiac.net*.

Garden Writers of America, 10210 Leatherleaf Court, Manassas, VA 20111; Tel: (703) 257-1032, Fax: (703) 257-0213.

✍ *www.gwaa.org*

Horror Writers Association (HWA), P.O. Box 50577, Palo Alto, CA 94303. E-mail: *hwa@horror.org*.

✍ *www.horror.org*

International Association of Crime Writers, North American Branch, P.O. Box 8674, New York, NY 10116-8674; Tel. and Fax: (212) 243-8966. E-mail: *mfrisquegc@apc.org*.

✍ *www.crimewritersna.org*

National Writers Association, 3140 S. Peoria Street, Suite 295, Aurora, CO 80014; Tel: (303) 841-0246. Presents annual conference.

✍ *www.nationalwriters.com*

Outdoor Writers Association of America.

✍ *www.owaa.org*

Overseas Press Club of America.

✍ *www.opcofamerica.org*

PEN (Poets, Playwrights, Essayists, Novelists), 568 Broadway, Suite 401, New York, NY 10012; Tel: (212) 334-1660; Fax: (212) 334-2181. E-mail: *pen@pen.org*; Web: *www.pen.org*. Western branch: PEN Center USA, West 672 S. Lafayette Park Place, Suite 42, Los Angeles, CA 90057; Tel: (213) 365-8500; Fax: (213) 365-9616. E-mail: *pen@pen-usa-west.org*; Web: *www.pen-usa-west.org*.

Poetry Society of America, 15 Gramercy Park W., New York, NY 10003; Tel: (212) 254-9628; Tel: (800) USA-POEM. E-mail: *poetrysocy@aol.com*.

✍ *www.poetrysociety.org*

Poets & Writers, 72 Spring Street, New York, NY 10012; Tel: (212) 226-3586; E-mail: *pwsubsw.org*.
✍ *www.pw.org*

Romance Writers of America (RWA), 16000 Stuebner Airline Road, Suite 140, Spring, TX 77379; Tel: (832) 717-5200. E-mail: *info@rwanational.com*.
✍ *www.rwanational.com*

Science Fiction & Fantasy Writers of America (SFWA). E-mail: *execdir@sfwa.org*.
✍ *www.sfwa.org*

Writers League of Texas, 1501 West Fifth Street, Suite E2, Austin, TX 78703; Tel: (512) 499-8914. E-mail: *awl@writersleague.org*. Presents programs, classes, workshops, contests, and supportive services for writers.
✍ *www.writersleague.org*

OTHER ORGANIZATIONS OF INTEREST TO WRITERS

American Booksellers Association, 828 S. Broadway, Suite 625, Tarrytown, NY 10591; Tel: (914) 591-2665; Tel: (800) 637-0037; Fax: (914) 591-2720. E-mail: *editorial@bookweb.org*. Publishes a monthly newsletter. Allied with regional associations. Sponsors ABA Convention and Trade Exhibit, held in conjunction with BEA.
✍ *www.bookweb.org*

BookExpo America (BEA), 383 Main Avenue, Norwalk, CT 06851; Tel: (203) 840-2840; Fax: (203) 840-9614. E-mail: *inquiry@bookexpo. reedexpo.com*.
✍ *www.bookexpo.reedexpo.com*

The Library of Congress, The Center for the Book, 101 Independence Avenue SE, Washington, DC 20540-4920; Tel: (202) 707-5221; Fax: (202) 707-0267. E-mail: *cfbook@loc.gov*. Presents exhibitions and events to stimulate interest in books and reading. Operates more than thirty affiliated state centers.

✑ *www.loc.gov/cfbook*

Friends of Libraries USA, 1420 Walnut Street, Suite 450, Philadelphia, PA 19102-4017; Tel: (215) 790-1674; Tel: (800) 936-5872; Fax: (215) 545-3821. E-mail: *folusa@libertynet.org.* Supports Friends of Libraries groups around the country.

✑ *www.folusa.com*

COPYRIGHT RESOURCES

U.S. Copyright Office—*www.copyright.gov*

Copyright Clearance Center—*www.copyright.com*

Index

About the Authors

Rick Frishman, president of Planned Television Arts since 1982, is one of the most powerful and energetic publicists in the media industry. In 1993 PTA merged with Ruder Finn, where Rick serves as an executive vice-president. While supervising PTA's success, he continues to work with many of the top editors, agents, and publishers in America including Simon & Schuster, Random House, HarperCollins, and Penguin Putnam. The authors he has worked with include Stephen King, President Jimmy Carter, Mark Victor Hansen, Henry Kissinger, and Jack Canfield.

Rick is a sought-after lecturer on publishing and public relations and is a member of PRSA and the National Speakers Association. He is co-host of the weekly radio show *Taking Care of Business*, which airs on WCWP in Long Island, New York *(www.tcbradio.com)*. Rick and his wife Robbi live in Long Island with their three children, Adam, Rachel, and Stephanie, and a cockapoo named Rusty.

Rick is the coauthor of *Guerrilla Marketing for Writers* and of the national bestseller *Guerrilla Publicity*. His book *Networking Magic* was released by Adams Media in 2004 and immediately went to #1 at Barnes&Noble.com.

Starting in 2006, he joins coauthor Robyn Spizman to travel the country under the banner of Author 101 University. You can e-mail Rick at *frishmanr@plannedtvarts.com,* or call him at (212) 593-5845. Visit *www.rickfrishman.com* for his Million Dollar Rolodex.

As an award-winning author, **Robyn Freedman Spizman** has written dozens of inspirational and educational nonfiction books, including *Make It Memorable, The GIFTionary, The Thank You Book,* and *When Words Matter Most.* Her first work of fiction, titled *Secret Agent,* is a novel for young adults. As a seasoned media personality and consumer advocate for more than twenty-three years, she has appeared repeatedly on NBC *Today, CNN Headline News,* and is featured regularly on the NBC's Atlanta affiliate WXIA and Star 94. A popular speaker nationally on book-writing and motivational topics, Spizman is considered one of the most dynamic how-to experts in the country. In addition to her writing, reporting, and speaking, she is the cofounder of The Spizman Agency, a highly successful public relations firm in Atlanta, Georgia, that specializes in book publicity. Robyn's Web site is *www.robynspizman.com.*

Announcing the Author 101

"Get Published, Get Publicized" CONTEST!

Ready to turn that great idea into a book proposal? Send it in and you could win a publishing **contract from Adams Media** and **$20,000 worth of publicity** from Planned Television Arts and the Spizman Agency!

For complete contest rules, visit:
http://www.author101.com/contest.html